Low Fat in Nothing Flat

Linda Rosensweig

A John Boswell Associates / King Hill Productions Book

HarperCollins*Publishers*

This book is dedicated to my daughters
Rachel and Samantha.

LOW FAT IN NOTHING FLAT.

HarperCollins books may be purchased for educational, business, or sales
promotional use. For information, please write: Special Markets Department,
HarperCollins Publishers, Inc., 10 East 53rd Street, New York, NY 10022.

Design: Richard Oriolo
Index: Maro Riofrancos

Library of Congress Cataloging-in-Publication Data

Rosensweig, Linda.
Low fat in nothing flat / Linda Rosensweig—1st ed.
p. cm.
"A John Boswell Associates/King Hill Productions book."
Includes index.
ISBN 0-06-017329-7

96 97 98 99 00 HC 10 9 8 7 6 5 4 3 2 1

Contents

Introduction

When people hear that I cook for a living, they often envision with envy our family sitting down to an elaborate multicourse dinner complete with all the trimmings. Invitations even for a single last-minute supper create expectations of an extravagant culinary feast laden with calories and fat. Well, they soon learn how wrong they are.

In point of fact, I'm a working mom with no time to be a slave to my kitchen, and I'm strongly committed to a reduced-fat diet. But I do have time to make sure that my family eats nutritionally sound food that is always tasty and sometimes downright elegant.

What really amazes people who dine in my home is just how flavorful the low-fat food they are eating is and how little time it took to whip up. "I can't believe it's so low-fat" and "You just got home—how did you do this so fast?" are the comments I hear over and over. That's what led me to create *Low Fat in Nothing Flat.* This book is written for people like you and me, with hectic lives, sophisticated tastes, and a strong inclination toward healthy eating. Whether we are married, single, with or without children, what we share is a desire for tasty, nourishing meals that are ready in no time flat.

Most of the recipes in this book can go from counter to table in 20 minutes or less. To achieve this, some require a little advance planning. I've taken advantage of quality convenience foods that save time: instant rice and refrigerated fresh pasta, precut broccoli florets and supermarket rotisserie chicken. Some recipes call for leftovers; never throw out the rice from your Chinese take-out. Minutes are shaved by "baking" potatoes in the microwave and shredding vegetables in the food processor. Of course, if you prefer, any of these dishes can be made with longer-cooking ingredients or by a more conventional method; just allow for the extra time.

A well-stocked pantry is essential to speedy recipe preparation. Having most of what you need on hand so you only have to shop for a few fresh items or specialty products saves even more time. Stocking your pantry with what I call "essentials" will take the worry out of everyday cooking because you'll know that you can always make a low-fat meal out of what you have on hand. The categories below are the ones I find most useful:

- Dried Goods—pasta, flour, dried fruits, cereals, and grains.
- Refrigerated Staples—skim milk, reduced-calorie margarine, nonfat yogurt, nonfat mayonnaise, nonfat sour cream, nonfat cream cheese, reduced- and low-fat cheese: Cheddar, Parmesan, and Swiss.
- Cans and Jars—canned beans, tunafish, corn niblets and other veg-

etables, reduced-sodium no-fat chicken broth, vegetable broth, fruit juices, evaporated skimmed milk, reduced-fat peanut butter.

- Sweeteners and Dessert Fixings—granulated sugar, brown sugar, confectioners' sugar, jams and preserves, vanilla and other flavorings, unsweetened cocoa powder.
- Oils and Vinegars—olive oil, vegetable oil, flavored vinegars, and don't forget the nonstick cooking spray.
- Condiments—roasted red peppers, olives, canned chopped green chiles, ketchup, Worcestershire sauce, hot pepper sauce.
- Herbs and Spices—imported bay leaves, dried thyme, oregano, rosemary, black peppercorns, grated nutmeg, etc.

Adapt these suggestions to your own likes and dislikes and, of course, to space limitations. A well-stocked pantry will make your meals infinitely easier and tastier.

Organization is the key to success in the kitchen. Getting organized not just in the pantry, but also with equipment, can cut your time in the kitchen in half. It is not necessary to stock your kitchen cabinets with all the latest in kitchenware, but several good pieces of cookware and certain appliances will make life much easier. For me, good nonstick cookware is one of the keys to quality low-fat cooking. I suggest a heavy 10- to 12-inch nonstick skillet, which is especially good for sautéing large amounts of vegetables and aromatics and for one-pot dishes, and a 6- to 8-inch skillet for omelets and smaller amounts of food. Three nonstick saucepans—small (1- to 1½-quart), medium (2- to 3½-quart), and large (3- to 5-quart), all with tight-fitting lids and preferably of stainless steel or some other nonreactive lining are a must. A large 4½- to 6-quart Dutch oven or other flameproof casserole is also used a lot. For low-fat stir-frying, you cannot beat a nonstick wok, which is definitely a worthwhile investment. Also needed are a couple of shallow ovenproof casseroles and baking dishes and a large nonstick baking sheet. A good set of sharp knives will save preparation time. I recommend a 4-inch paring knife, a 6-inch all-purpose knife, and an 8- to 10-inch chef's knife for cutting and chopping. The best knives are made from high carbon steel mixed with stainless steel.

Appliances are a very personal thing. Some people like to have every gadget ever made and others can get by with a simple chef's knife. I fall somewhere in between. For this book, with just a few pieces of equipment—food processor, microwave oven, and either a standing or handheld electric mixer—you can tackle most any recipe. Of course, if space and budget permit, some specialty appliances can save valuable extra minutes. A mini food processor, for example, is great for chopping a couple of tablespoons of parsley or mincing a couple of garlic cloves in an instant.

The following recipes cover the gamut, offering low-fat dishes you can combine into nutritional menus for any meal of the day, from breakfasts and between-meal snacks to lunch and dinner. There are soups, starters and pastas, main courses, side dishes, and desserts. My hope is that *Low Fat in Nothing Flat* will show you just how easy it can be to eat healthy and serve your family delicious homemade food in the time you have at hand.

Breakfast
on the Fly

Breakfast is a very personal meal. Some people can't start the day without a full meal in the morning; others want simply a caffeine jump start. Whether you are someone who prefers a lighter bite or a full pancake breakfast, this chapter will have a low-fat recipe to suit your taste.

All research points to breakfast as being the most important meal of the day. It gets your system up and going and reduces the craving for a mid-morning snack. So even if you lean toward less when you get up, try not to skip breakfast completely. If a lighter bite is what you desire, consider starting with a Creamy Banana Shake. Pack some Quick Apple Muesli in a small sealable snack bag, and open it later, when your appetite kicks in.

I've also included a number of lovely low-fat recipes that would make a delightful brunch: Zucchini Cheese Frittata, Breakfast Lemon Rice Parfaits, Speedy Herbed Hash Browns. But because these dishes are so quick as well as so lean, you don't have to save them for weekends.

Included in this chapter are recipes that can suit your every morning need. From sweet to savory, to meals suited for a weekend brunch, there is a recipe here for you. With all these options there is no excuse for skipping this all-important meal.

Dried Fruit Couscous

Makes 4 servings

Couscous is a great handy grain to add to your pantry. Here dried fruit and cinnamon turn it into a mildly sweet breakfast treat.

1 cup orange juice

¼ cup apple juice

¼ cup golden raisins

¼ cup finely chopped dried apricots

¼ cup finely chopped dried apples

1 cinnamon stick

¾ cup quick-cooking couscous

1 tablespoon grated orange zest

⅓ cup nonfat vanilla-flavored yogurt

1 tablespoon honey

1. In a medium saucepan, combine orange juice, apple juice, raisins, dried apricots and apples, and cinnamon stick. Bring to a boil. Stir in couscous and orange zest. Remove from heat. Cover and let stand 5 minutes.

2. In a small bowl, mix yogurt and honey. Fluff couscous with a fork; remove and discard cinnamon stick.

3. Divide couscous among 4 bowls. Top each with a large dollop of honeyed yogurt. Serve at once.

PER SERVING   Calories 260   Total Fat <1 g   Saturated Fat <1 g
Cholesterol 0 mg   Percentage calories from fat 0%

Quick Apple Muesli

Makes 4 servings; approximately 4 cups

½ cup skim milk

¼ cup quick-cooking oats

¼ cup nonfat vanilla-flavored yogurt

2 medium apples

1 medium pear

½ cup orange-pineapple juice

2 tablespoons ground pecans

2 tablespoons honey

1 tablespoon grated orange zest

½ teaspoon cinnamon

1 medium banana, thinly sliced

½ cup blueberries

1. In a large bowl, combine milk, oats, and yogurt. Mix well. Let stand 5 minutes.

2. Meanwhile, without peeling, halve apples and pear and scoop out cores. Coarsely grate on shredding disk of a food processor or shred on large holes of a hand grater.

3. Stir juice, pecans, honey, orange zest, and cinnamon into oat mixture until well blended. Mix in shredded fruit, banana, and blueberries. Serve at once.

PER SERVING   Calories 204   Total Fat 3 g   Saturated Fat <1 g
Cholesterol 1 mg   Percentage calories from fat 12%

Banana French Toast

Makes 4 servings

Cinnamon and banana make this a great treat. Serve with maple syrup or with Maple Fruit Topping (recipe follows).

¾ cup egg substitute

½ cup skim milk

½ cup mashed banana

1 teaspoon sugar

½ teaspoon cinnamon

8 slices French bread, cut ¾ inch thick

1 tablespoon reduced-calorie margarine

1. In a shallow bowl or pie plate, whisk together egg substitute, milk, banana, sugar, and cinnamon until well blended. Add bread slices and soak briefly on both sides.

2. Coat a large nonstick skillet with nonstick cooking spray. Melt margarine in skillet over medium heat. Add bread slices in batches and cook, turning, until golden brown, 3 to 4 minutes on each side. Serve at once.

PER SERVING   Calories 233   Total Fat 4 g   Saturated Fat 1 g
Cholesterol 1 mg   Percentage calories from fat 14%

Maple Fruit Topping

Makes 4 servings; approximately 2 cups

This topping can be used for many breakfast foods, including pancakes, waffles, and French toast. Reduced-calorie pancake syrup is a great way to enjoy that maple taste without the added calories.

2 teaspoons reduced-calorie margarine
1 large apple, peeled and chopped
½ teaspoon cinnamon
Pinch nutmeg
½ cup unsweetened apple juice
⅓ cup reduced-calorie pancake syrup or maple syrup
1 tablespoon fresh lemon juice

1. In a medium saucepan, melt margarine over medium heat. Add apples, cinnamon, and nutmeg. Cook, stirring often, 4 to 5 minutes, until apples are tender.

2. Stir in apple juice, pancake syrup, and lemon juice. Bring to a boil. Reduce heat to low and simmer 5 minutes, stirring occasionally. Serve warm.

PER SERVING   Calories 74   Total Fat 1 g   Saturated Fat <1 g
Cholesterol 0 mg   Percentage calories from fat 13%

Crunchy French Toast

Makes 4 servings

A twist on typical French toast, this version adds a crunchy coating to the bread. Serve with Dried Apple-Pear Butter (recipe follows). For a change, try using reduced-calorie raisin bread in place of the whole grain bread suggested here.

> 4 cups bran flakes or cornflakes cereal
> ½ cup egg substitute
> 2 tablespoons orange juice
> 2 tablespoons skim milk
> 4 slices reduced-calorie whole grain bread

1. Coat a broiler pan or indoor ridged grill pan with nonstick cooking spray. Preheat broiler or grill pan. Place cereal flakes in a heavy-duty plastic bag and crush with a rolling pin to form fine crumbs. Or grind in a food processor. Place crumbs on a large sheet of wax paper.

2. In a shallow bowl or pie plate, combine egg substitute, orange juice, and milk. Beat with a fork to mix well. One at a time, dip bread slices in egg mixture to moisten evenly. Dredge in cereal crumbs to coat on both sides.

3. Broil toasts about 6 inches from heat or grill over medium heat 2 to 4 minutes on each side, until golden brown.

PER SERVING   Calories 194   Total Fat 1 g   Saturated Fat <1 g
Cholesterol <1 mg   Percentage calories from fat 5%

Dried Apple-Pear Butter

*L*ean *apple-pear butter is great to have on hand to spread on toast or muffins in place of fatty butter or cream cheese. It's also nice to spoon into decorative jars and give as gifts for the holidays.*

1 cup apple juice
1 cup unsweetened pineapple juice
1 cup dried apple slices
1 cup dried pear slices
1 teaspoon cinnamon
¼ teaspoon allspice
Pinch cloves

1. In a medium saucepan, combine all ingredients. Bring to a boil. Reduce heat to low, cover, and simmer 15 minutes, stirring occasionally.

2. Transfer fruit mixture to a food processor and puree until smooth. Serve warm or cover and refrigerate for later use.

PER TABLESPOON   Calories 118   Total Fat <1 g   Saturated Fat 0 g
Cholesterol 0 mg   Percentage calories from fat 2%

Banana Raisin Pancakes

Makes 4 servings

Make sure the bananas are very ripe for this recipe, or the pancakes will not be as sweet as they should be. These can also be held in a warm oven for up to half an hour if you are not planning to serve them right away. If the pancakes begin to stick to the skillet, coat the pan with nonstick spray.

½ cup oat flour blend
1 tablespoon finely ground walnuts
2 teaspoons brown sugar
¼ teaspoon salt
¼ teaspoon cinnamon
3 large ripe bananas
2 large egg whites
2 tablespoons skim milk
2 teaspoons fresh lemon juice
½ cup raisins, dark or golden
2 teaspoons vegetable oil

1. In a medium bowl, combine flour, walnuts, sugar, salt, and cinnamon. Mix well.

2. In a medium bowl, mash bananas. Blend in egg whites, milk, and lemon juice; mix well. Stir in flour mixture just until combined. Gently stir in raisins.

3. Heat oil in a large nonstick skillet. Add batter by ¼ cupfuls to skillet and cook, turning once, until golden on both sides, 2 to 4 minutes on each side.

PER SERVING   Calories 243   Total Fat 4 g   Saturated Fat 1 g
Cholesterol 0 mg   Percentage calories from fat 14%

Nutty Pancakes

Makes 4 servings

1 cup flour
1 tablespoon brown sugar
1 teaspoon baking powder
½ cup nonfat plain yogurt
½ cup skim milk
¼ cup egg substitute
½ teaspoon vanilla extract
2 tablespoons finely chopped almonds
2 teaspoons reduced-calorie margarine
Confectioners' sugar

1. In a large bowl, combine flour, brown sugar, and baking powder. In a medium bowl, mix together yogurt, milk, egg substitute, and vanilla until blended. Gently stir yogurt mixture into dry ingredients just until combined. Stir in almonds.

2. Melt margarine in a large nonstick skillet over medium heat. Drop batter by scant ¼ cupfuls into skillet. Cook 2 to 3 minutes on each side, until golden.

3. Top with a dusting of confectioners' sugar and serve hot.

PER SERVING   Calories 197   Total Fat 4 g   Saturated Fat 1 g
Cholesterol 1 mg   Percentage calories from fat 17%

Zucchini Cheese Frittata

Makes 4 servings

Egg whites replace the whole eggs in this recipe for a real cholesterol savings. The frittata also works nicely as a light dinner.

¾ teaspoon olive oil

¾ cup shredded zucchini

½ cup chopped scallions

2 garlic cloves, minced

8 large egg whites

½ teaspoon dried basil

¼ teaspoon paprika

¼ teaspoon salt

Pinch ground white pepper

2 tablespoons grated provolone cheese

1. Preheat broiler. Coat a large nonstick skillet with a flameproof handle with nonstick cooking spray. Heat oil in skillet over medium-high heat. Add zucchini, scallions, and garlic. Cook, stirring often, until zucchini is tender, 4 to 5 minutes. Remove to a plate and let cool slightly.

2. In a large bowl, whisk together egg whites, basil, paprika, salt, and pepper until frothy and well blended. Stir in zucchini mixture.

3. Return skillet to medium heat. Add egg white-zucchini mixture and cook without stirring, until eggs begin to brown at edges, about 3 minutes. Cover pan and cook 3 minutes longer, or until frittata is just set.

4. Sprinkle cheese evenly over frittata. Place skillet under broiler 6 to 8 inches from heat and broil 1 to 2 minutes, until frittata is puffed and golden.

PER SERVING   Calories 66   Total Fat 2 g   Saturated Fat 1 g
Cholesterol 2 mg   Percentage calories from fat 29%

Bacon and Egg Pockets

Makes 4 servings

This recipe will keep you out of the fast-food restaurants for breakfast and save you cholesterol, and many fat grams and calories at the same time.

2 strips turkey bacon

1 teaspoon reduced-calorie margarine

1 medium green bell pepper, cut into thin strips

1 medium red onion, thinly sliced and separated into rings

½ teaspoon dried basil

¼ teaspoon dried oregano

1 cup egg substitute

½ cup skim milk

¼ teaspoon salt

¼ teaspoon freshly ground black pepper

2 (6-inch) pita breads, cut in half

1. In a large nonstick skillet, cook bacon over medium heat, turning, until crisp, about 5 minutes. Drain on paper towels. Crumble bacon.

2. Melt margarine in same skillet. Add bell pepper, onion, basil, and oregano. Cook, stirring often, until vegetables are soft, 4 to 5 minutes.

3. In a medium bowl, beat together egg substitute, milk, salt, and pepper until blended. Pour over vegetables in skillet and cook, stirring often, until eggs thicken but are not set, 3 to 4 minutes. Stir in bacon and continue cooking, stirring, until the eggs are no longer runny, 1 to 2 minutes longer.

4. Stuff bacon and eggs into pita pockets and serve at once.

PER SERVING   Calories 166   Total Fat 2 g   Saturated Fat <1 g
Cholesterol 6 mg   Percentage calories from fat 12%

Muffin Pizza Omelet

Makes 4 servings

For breakfast or brunch, you can't beat this substantial dish, which uses many of the toppings you'd find on your favorite pizza. To save on cholesterol and fat, egg whites replace some whole eggs and nonfat cheese replaces the regular variety.

6 large egg whites

2 whole eggs

½ teaspoon dried basil

¼ teaspoon salt

¼ teaspoon freshly ground black pepper

1 large plum tomato, seeded and chopped

¼ cup shredded nonfat mozzarella cheese

2 ounces turkey pepperoni, thinly sliced

4 English muffins, split and toasted

1. In a medium bowl, whisk together egg whites, whole eggs, basil, salt, and pepper until well blended.

2. Coat a large nonstick skillet with nonstick cooking spray. Heat skillet over medium heat. Add one-fourth of egg mixture and cook without stirring 2 to 3 minutes, until eggs are almost set.

3. Sprinkle one-fourth of tomatoes, cheese, and pepperoni over eggs. Cook until eggs are set, 1 to 2 minutes longer. Fold omelet in half and slide onto 2 English muffin halves on a plate.

4. Repeat to make 3 more omelets, spraying skillet again if needed to prevent sticking.

PER SERVING   Calories 172   Total Fat 5 g   Saturated Fat 2 g
Cholesterol 118 mg   Percentage calories from fat 2%

Speedy Herbed Hash Browns

Makes 4 servings

4 cups frozen shredded potatoes

½ cup grated onion

½ teaspoon salt

½ teaspoon dried thyme

¼ teaspoon paprika

¼ teaspoon freshly ground black pepper

Pinch crumbled rosemary

2 teaspoons canola oil

1. Place potatoes in a medium microwave-safe glass or ceramic bowl, cover, and microwave on high 1 minute, or until slightly thawed.

2. Blend in onion, salt, thyme, paprika, pepper, and rosemary. Mix well to break up potatoes.

3. Coat a large nonstick skillet with nonstick cooking spray. Heat oil in skillet over medium heat. Add potato mixture and cook, stirring often, until potatoes are golden and tender, 6 to 8 minutes.

PER SERVING   Calories 203   Total Fat 4 g   Saturated Fat 1 g
Cholesterol 0 mg   Percentage calories from fat 17%

Breakfast Rice Stir-Fry

Makes 4 servings

Here is a tasty dish similar to the fried rice you would find in a Chinese restaurant. It makes for a welcome change at the breakfast table. Like typical fried rice, it is designed to use up leftovers from dinner. A reduced amount of oil and low-fat ham really help to keep down the fat grams in this recipe.

2 teaspoons olive oil

½ cup chopped onion

2 cups cooked rice, white or brown

¼ cup shredded carrot

1 cup egg substitute

½ cup chopped low-fat smoked ham

Salt and freshly ground black pepper

1 tablespoon chopped fresh parsley

1. In a large wok or nonstick skillet, heat oil over medium-high heat. Add onion and stir-fry 2 minutes. Add rice and carrot and cook, stirring constantly, 2 to 3 minutes, until rice is golden.

2. Add egg substitute and ham to skillet. Cook, stirring constantly, 3 to 4 minutes, until eggs are set.

3. Season with salt and pepper to taste. Garnish with chopped parsley and serve.

PER SERVING Calories 178 Total Fat 3 g Saturated Fat 1 g
Cholesterol 8 mg Percentage calories from fat 18%

Breakfast Lemon Rice Parfaits

Makes 4 servings

I *always make this for breakfast when I have some leftover rice from the night before. If you don't have any and you still have a craving for this breakfast treat, whip up some instant rice and let it cool slightly before beginning.*

1 cup nonfat lemon-flavored yogurt

1 ¼ cups cooked rice, chilled

1 cup coarsely chopped canned unsweetened peaches

1 cup thinly sliced strawberries

1 cup thinly sliced bananas

¼ cup honey- or regular-flavored wheat germ

½ teaspoon cinnamon

1. In a medium bowl, combine yogurt, rice, and peaches. Stir lightly to mix.

2. Spoon layers of the rice mixture, strawberries, and bananas into 4 large wineglasses.

3. Before serving, sprinkle 1 tablespoon wheat germ and ⅛ teaspoon cinnamon on top of each.

PER SERVING   Calories 236   Total Fat 1 g   Saturated Fat <1 g
Cholesterol 0 mg   Percentage calories from fat 5%

Peanut Butter Yogurt Spread

Makes 8 servings; approximately 1 ½ cups

If you love peanut butter, as I do, you can't help but be thrilled with the new reduced-fat versions that are readily available. Here it's blended with other nonfat ingredients to make a light but tasty spread that's great on everything from bagels to biscuits.

1 cup Yogurt Cheese (recipe follows)
¼ cup reduced-fat peanut butter
2 tablespoons nonfat plain yogurt
2 tablespoons plus 1 teaspoon honey
1 teaspoon vanilla extract

In a small food processor or by hand, combine all ingredients and blend until smooth. Cover and refrigerate if not using right away. This spread keeps well for up to 5 days.

PER SERVING   Calories 99   Total Fat 3 g   Saturated Fat 1 g
Cholesterol 0 mg   Percentage calories from fat 30%

Yogurt Cheese

Makes about 1 cup

*W*hile most of the recipes in this book are ready in a flash, this one does take a few hours to set up. However, all you have to do is spoon out the yogurt, so the actual preparation time is minimal. Fancy yogurt strainers are available but I find that regular coffee filters work just as well. Yogurt cheese is a great nonfat substitute for cream cheese. It can also be flavored with herbs and garlic and used as a spread or dip.

2 cups (1 pint) nonfat plain yogurt

1. Place a coffee filter in a small stainless steel or plastic strainer and set over a bowl. Spoon yogurt into filter.

2. Place bowl in refrigerator and let drain 3 hours, or overnight, until "cheese" is firm, and most of watery whey has dripped into bowl.

TIP: Whey—which is tart, nutritious, and nonfat—can be added to soups. Used in place of water in piecrusts, it enhances flakiness.

PER ¼ CUP   Calories 40   Total Fat 0 g   Saturated Fat 0 g
Cholesterol 0 mg   Percentage calories from fat 0%

Creamy Banana Shake

Makes 4 servings

Tofu is a great way to add creaminess to a shake and add protein at the same time. Make sure to squeeze the tofu dry before using, or the shake will become too watery.

½ pound soft tofu

1 large ripe banana, sliced

2 cups mixed tropical juice blend

1 cup canned crushed pineapple

½ cup crushed ice

2 tablespoons honey-flavored wheat germ

¼ teaspoon pure almond extract

1. Gently squeeze tofu in a clean kitchen towel to remove as much moisture as possible. Transfer to a blender or food processor.

2. Add all remaining ingredients. Blend until smooth. Serve right away.

PER SERVING   Calories 178   Total Fat 2 g   Saturated Fat <1 g
Cholesterol 0 mg   Percentage calories from fat 10%

Speedy Snacks and Starters

Let's face it, we all love to snack. Unfortunately, with today's rushed and hectic lifestyles, snack food has been lumped into the fast-food category, often sacrificing sound nutrition for the sake of ease. This chapter provides plenty of healthy choices before you reach for that commercially prepared high-fat quick fix. Here you'll also find light dips, spreads, and pickups to serve as starters or appetizers when you entertain. Often the distinction between a snack and a starter is blurred. Savory Lemon Hummus, for example, offers a tasty, low-fat treat whether it's served at a party as a dip with pita wedges or crudités or at home to keep you away from the chips and cookies in the late afternoon or in front of the VCR in the late evening.

A little planning can keep off pounds while it saves you a trip to the local convenience store. Plan ahead and bake a batch of Fruit-Filled Mini Muffins or Garlic Baked Potato Chips. They both will keep for several days and are a great addition to lunch boxes and brown bags. Many of these tempting bites can also double as a light evening meal when you just feel like something small yet satisfying. Perfect for this role are Chive Pancakes with Dipping Sauce, Cheesy Broiled Crostini, and South-of-the-Border Vegetable Nachos. Regardless of how you use these recipes, you can enjoy them guilt-free knowing they are all low-fat and ready in nothing flat.

Chunky Salsa with Feta Cheese

Makes 4 servings

You can vary the flavor of this salsa a bit by using different-flavored feta cheeses. If only plain is available, stir in some coarsely cracked black pepper or a hefty pinch of thyme and oregano. Serve with fat-free tortilla chips or mini rice cakes.

1 (14½-ounce) can diced tomatoes, drained

½ cup drained canned Mexican-style corn

¼ cup chopped red onion

¼ cup crumbled herb-flavored feta cheese

1 tablespoon lime juice

¼ teaspoon ground cumin

2 to 3 drops hot pepper sauce, or more to taste

In a medium bowl, combine all ingredients. Stir to mix well.

PER SERVING   Calories 65   Total Fat 2 g   Saturated Fat 1 g
Cholesterol 6 mg   Percentage calories from fat 28%

Apricot Chutney Dip

Makes 12 servings; approximately 1¼ cups

This is a great dip to have on hand for late afternoon snack attacks. For a low-fat serving suggestion, try nonfat pepper-flavored crackers or pear and apple wedges.

⅔ cup nonfat ricotta cheese

6 dried apricot halves

3 tablespoons nonfat cream cheese

2 tablespoons orange juice

½ teaspoon grated lemon zest

¼ teaspoon curry powder

¼ cup chutney

1. In a food processor, combine ricotta cheese, dried apricots, cream cheese, orange juice, and lemon zest. Puree until most of dip is smooth, with small pieces of apricot still visible.

2. Add curry powder and process until well blended.

3. Remove dip to a small bowl. Stir in chutney until combined.

PER SERVING   Calories 34   Total Fat 0 g   Saturated Fat 0 g
Cholesterol 1 mg   Percentage calories from fat 0%

White Bean and Pepper Dip

Makes 12 servings

This flavor-packed dip is great to take on picnics. Serve either with fresh vegetables or with pepper-flavored fat-free crackers.

- 2 teaspoons olive oil
- 1 medium red onion, finely chopped
- 2 garlic cloves, minced
- 1 (15-ounce) can cannellini or other white beans, rinsed and drained
- 1 (7-ounce) jar roasted red peppers, drained and chopped
- ¼ cup minced celery
- 2 tablespoons chopped flat-leaf parsley
- 2 teaspoons red wine vinegar

1. In a small nonstick skillet, heat oil over medium heat. Add red onion and garlic and cook, stirring frequently, until softened, 3 to 5 minutes.

2. In a medium bowl, partially mash beans with a fork. Stir in red onion and garlic, roasted peppers, celery, parsley, and vinegar. Mix well.

PER SERVING Calories 43 Total Fat 1 g Saturated Fat <1 g
Cholesterol 0 mg Percentage calories from fat 20%

Savory Lemon Hummus

Makes 12 servings

This garlicky chickpea dip is great served with pieces of pita bread or with fresh vegetables. Try whole wheat pitas for a change. Make sure to drain the chickpeas first or the hummus will be very thin.

1 (15-ounce) can chickpeas, drained
¼ cup fresh cilantro leaves
2 tablespoons nonfat plain yogurt
2½ tablespoons fresh lemon juice
1 tablespoon tahini or smooth reduced-fat peanut butter
2 garlic cloves, crushed
1 teaspoon ground cumin
¼ teaspoon cayenne
¼ cup finely chopped scallions
3 (6-inch) pita breads, cut into wedges

1. In a food processor, combine chickpeas, cilantro, yogurt, lemon juice, tahini, garlic, cumin, cayenne, and 2 tablespoons water. Puree until hummus is smooth.

2. To serve, spoon hummus into a serving bowl. Sprinkle scallions over top. Serve with pita wedges for dipping.

PER SERVING   Calories 78   Total Fat 1 g   Saturated Fat <1 g
Cholesterol 0 mg   Percentage calories from fat 17%

Cheesy Broiled Crostini

Makes 8 servings

These little bread toasts serve as a welcome start to any dinner. They also make a terrific hot appetizer. The earthy flavor of balsamic vinegar gives the filling a nice boost.

1 cup nonfat ricotta cheese
¾ cup Italian-flavored dry bread crumbs
¼ cup egg substitute
¼ cup chopped roasted red pepper
1 tablespoon shredded provolone cheese
1 teaspoon balsamic vinegar
½ teaspoon dried basil
¼ teaspoon garlic powder
24 slices stale whole grain French bread, cut ½ inch thick
¼ teaspoon paprika

1. Preheat broiler. In a small bowl, combine ricotta cheese, bread crumbs, egg substitute, red pepper, provolone cheese, vinegar, basil, and garlic powder. Mix to blend well.

2. Place bread slices on a large baking sheet. Spread approximately 1 tablespoon ricotta topping over each. Dust with paprika.

3. Broil about 6 inches from heat until topping is bubbly, 3 to 5 minutes. Serve warm.

PER SERVING   Calories 119   Total Fat 1 g   Saturated Fat <1 g
Cholesterol 1 mg   Percentage calories from fat 8%

Mozzarella Tomato Crostini

Makes 4 servings

A perfect recipe to make in the summer months when fresh tomatoes are in abundance. For a change, try using smoked mozzarella instead of regular.

2 teaspoons olive oil

1 teaspoon balsamic vinegar

½ teaspoon dried basil

½ teaspoon dried oregano

¼ teaspoon salt

¼ teaspoon freshly ground black pepper

4 slices Italian bread, cut ½ inch thick

2 ripe plum tomatoes, cut into 4 thick slices each

1½ ounces reduced-fat mozzarella cheese, cut into 8 thin slices

1 tablespoon grated Parmesan cheese

1. Preheat broiler. In a small bowl, whisk together olive oil, vinegar, basil, oregano, salt, and pepper.

2. Place bread slices on a large baking sheet. Broil 1 minute, or until lightly toasted on one side. Turn bread over and top each with 2 tomato slices. Brush seasoned oil evenly over tomatoes. Broil 2 to 3 minutes, until tomatoes start to sizzle.

3. Place a mozzarella slice on top of each tomato slice. Sprinkle evenly with Parmesan cheese. Broil 2 to 3 minutes longer, until cheese begins to melt.

PER SERVING   Calories 149   Total Fat 5 g   Saturated Fat 1 g
Cholesterol 4 mg   Percentage calories from fat 30%

South-of-the-Border Vegetable Nachos

Makes 4 servings

Calories in this very popular dish are reduced by substituting bell pepper strips for the taco chips. Top them with your favorite low-fat Mexican treats.

    4 medium bell peppers (preferably 2 green and 2 red), cut into
        1½-inch strips
    1 medium tomato, finely chopped
    1 (4-ounce) can chopped green chiles
    3 tablespoons chopped fresh cilantro
    ¼ teaspoon crushed hot red pepper
    ⅓ cup shredded reduced-fat Monterey Jack cheese
    ⅓ cup shredded reduced-fat Cheddar cheese
    ½ cup nonfat sour cream

1. Preheat broiler. Place pepper strips close together in a shallow baking dish. Top each with equal amounts of tomato, chiles, cilantro, and hot pepper. Sprinkle cheeses on top.

2. Broil about 6 inches from heat for 3 minutes, or until cheese melts and is bubbly. Serve topped with dollops of sour cream.

PER SERVING   Calories 110   Total Fat 4 g   Saturated Fat 2 g
Cholesterol 13 mg   Percentage calories from fat 29%

Crunchy Chicken Fingers

Makes 4 servings

¼ cup egg substitute

2 tablespoons nonfat plain yogurt

¾ cup bran flakes cereal

2 tablespoons yellow cornmeal

1 tablespoon cheese-flavored sprinkles

1 tablespoon grated reduced-fat Parmesan cheese

⅛ teaspoon dry mustard

⅛ teaspoon salt

Pinch cayenne

½ pound skinless boneless chicken breast, cut crosswise into
⅓-inch-wide strips

1. Preheat oven to 400 degrees F. Spray a large baking sheet with nonstick cooking spray. In a shallow bowl, combine egg substitute and yogurt. Whisk until well blended.

2. In a food processor, combine cereal, cornmeal, sprinkles, Parmesan cheese, mustard, salt, and cayenne. Process until ground to fine crumbs. Transfer to another shallow bowl or a sheet of wax paper.

3. Dip chicken strips in yogurt mixture, then dredge in crumbs to coat all over. Place on prepared baking sheet.

4. Bake chicken 12 to 15 minutes, turning once, until golden brown outside and white in center.

PER SERVING   Calories 124   Total Fat 1 g   Saturated Fat <1 g
Cholesterol 34 mg   Percentage calories from fat: 10%

Chive Pancakes with Dipping Sauce

Makes 4 servings

I modeled this recipe after the scallion pancakes found in Chinese restaurants. Here the pancakes are loaded with chives, and the scallions are found in a light gingery sauce.

2 tablespoons soy sauce

2 tablespoons rice wine vinegar

2 tablespoons minced scallions

2 teaspoons grated fresh ginger

½ teaspoon peanut oil

¾ cup all-purpose flour

¾ cup skim milk

¼ cup egg substitute

2 tablespoons chicken broth or water

¼ teaspoon ground ginger

Pinch Chinese five-spice powder

½ cup finely chopped chives or scallion greens

1 teaspoon baking powder

1. In a small bowl, combine soy sauce, vinegar, scallions, fresh ginger, and peanut oil. Set the ginger sauce aside.

2. In a blender or food processor, combine flour, milk, egg substitute, broth, ginger, and five-spice powder. Puree until smooth. Transfer batter to a bowl and let stand 2 minutes. Stir in chives and baking powder. Mix well.

3. Spray a large nonstick griddle or skillet with nonstick spray; heat over medium heat. Pour batter by tablespoons into skillet to make 4 small pancakes. Cook until bubbles appear on top, 1 to 2 minutes. Turn pancakes over and cook 30 seconds longer.

4. Remove pancakes to a platter and cover to keep warm. Repeat with remaining batter to make 16 pancakes. Serve warm, with ginger sauce for dipping.

PER SERVING   Calories 132   Total Fat 2 g   Saturated Fat <1 g
Cholesterol 1 mg   Percentage calories from fat 13%

Garlic Baked Potato Chips

Makes 8 servings

3 tablespoons grated reduced-fat Parmesan cheese
½ teaspoon garlic powder
½ teaspoon paprika
½ teaspoon ground cumin
½ teaspoon salt
Pinch cayenne
½ pound baking potatoes, scrubbed
½ pound sweet potatoes, scrubbed

1. Preheat oven to 300 degrees F. Spray a large baking sheet with nonstick cooking spray. In a small bowl, combine Parmesan cheese, garlic powder, paprika, cumin, salt, and cayenne. Mix well.

2. With a large sharp knife or food processor fitted with slicing blade, cut potatoes and sweet potatoes into very thin slices. Arrange on prepared baking sheet in a single layer.

3. Sprinkle slices on both sides with cheese mixture. Bake 10 to 12 minutes, until chips are golden brown and crispy.

PER SERVING   Calories 61   Total Fat 1 g   Saturated Fat <1 g
Cholesterol 1 mg   Percentage calories from fat 8%

Crispy Potato Skins

Makes 4 servings

*S*tarting *with leftover baked potatoes makes this a real time-saver; just bake a couple of extra potatoes the night before. In no time flat you can have a savory low-fat snack. Tip: If you forgot to bake extra potatoes, zap these in the microwave for 6 to 8 minutes on high before beginning.*

2 cooked large baking potatoes

1 ½ tablespoons olive oil

2 garlic cloves, crushed

1 teaspoon salt-free lemon-herb seasoning blend

1 teaspoon butter-flavored sprinkles

¼ teaspoon paprika

¼ teaspoon salt

1 tablespoon grated provolone cheese

1. Preheat broiler. Cut potatoes lengthwise into quarters. Scoop out potatoes, leaving a ¼-inch shell of skin. Reserve insides for another use.

2. In a small bowl, combine oil, garlic, seasoning blend, butter sprinkles, paprika, and salt. Brush over both sides of potato shells. Place potatoes skin side down on a large baking sheet.

3. Sprinkle cheese evenly over skins. Broil 3 to 5 minutes, until browned and crispy.

PER SERVING   Calories 181   Total Fat 6 g   Saturated Fat 1 g
Cholesterol 1 mg   Percentage calories from fat 28%

"Candied" Apples

Makes 4 servings

Kids *love this healthful sweet snack, which can double as dessert. Pears also work well, but be sure to choose a firm variety and broil them the minimum amount of time.*

2 Red Delicious apples, halved, cored, and sliced

2 tablespoons fresh lemon juice

2 tablespoons reduced-calorie margarine

1 tablespoon dark brown sugar

½ teaspoon vanilla extract

¼ teaspoon cinnamon

1. Preheat broiler. Spray a baking sheet with nonstick cooking spray. Arrange apple slices, overlapping, in rows on prepared baking sheet. Sprinkle lemon juice over apples.

2. In a small saucepan, combine margarine, brown sugar, vanilla, and cinnamon. Cook over low heat, stirring occasionally, until margarine and brown sugar are melted, about 2 minutes. Brush evenly over apples.

3. Broil about 6 inches from heat 3 to 5 minutes, until glazed and golden. Let cool slightly before eating.

PER SERVING   Calories 94   Total Fat 3 g   Saturated Fat 1 g
Cholesterol 0 mg   Percentage calories from fat 30%

Fruit-Filled Mini Muffins

Makes 12 servings

*A*ny *berries can be substituted for the strawberries. For larger muffins, spoon the filling into twelve 2¾ -inch muffin cups. The baking time will be slightly longer. Serve with your favorite preserves or all-fruit spread.*

2 cups all-purpose flour

⅓ cup sugar

¼ cup yellow cornmeal

1 tablespoon grated orange zest

1 teaspoon baking powder

1 teaspoon baking soda

1 cup nonfat plain yogurt

2 large egg whites

2½ tablespoons margarine, melted

¼ cup orange juice

1½ teaspoons vanilla extract

1 cup finely chopped strawberries

1. Preheat oven to 400 degrees F. Spray 24 mini muffin cups with nonstick cooking spray.

2. In a large bowl, combine flour, sugar, cornmeal, orange zest, baking powder, and baking soda. Stir or whisk gently to mix. In a medium bowl, combine yogurt, egg whites, margarine, orange juice, and vanilla. Blend well. Add liquid ingredients to dry; mix just until combined. Gently stir in strawberries.

3. Spoon batter evenly into prepared cups to fill about two-thirds full. Bake 10 to 12 minutes, until a toothpick inserted in center comes out clean. Remove muffins immediately from pan. Serve warm.

PER MUFFIN   Calories 153   Total Fat 3 g   Saturated Fat <1 g
Cholesterol 0 mg   Percentage calories from fat 18%

Candy Bar Rice Cake Crunch

Makes 4 servings

This satisfying snack is made to taste like the "real" thing. Rice crackers make a great fat-free base for this quick treat.

2 teaspoons shredded unsweetened coconut

4 teaspoons reduced-fat peanut butter

4 large caramel-flavored rice cakes

¼ cup crispy rice cereal

1 tablespoon reduced-calorie chocolate-flavored syrup

1. In a small dry skillet, cook coconut over medium-high heat, stirring constantly, until lightly toasted, 1 to 2 minutes. Remove to a small bowl and set aside.

2. Spread 1 teaspoon peanut butter over each rice cake. Sprinkle 1 tablespoon cereal over each; pat gently with back of a spoon to help stick.

3. Drizzle equal amounts of chocolate syrup over each rice cake and sprinkle coconut on top.

PER SERVING   Calories 99   Total Fat 2 g   Saturated Fat 1 g
Cholesterol 0 mg   Percentage calories from fat 21%

Cinnamon Rice Crunch Mix

Makes 8 servings

Most dried banana slices contain added fat. Look for those that do not. If your supermarket doesn't have them, a health food store will.

3 tablespoons dark brown sugar

2 tablespoons reduced-calorie margarine

2 tablespoons unsweetened apple juice concentrate

1 ¼ teaspoons cinnamon

5 ½ cups puffed rice or wheat cereal

1 cup coarsely chopped dried apple slices

½ cup dried banana slices

1 tablespoon honey-flavored wheat germ

1. Preheat oven to 250 degrees F. Place sugar, margarine, juice concentrate, and cinnamon in 13 by 9-inch baking dish. Set in oven and heat 1 to 2 minutes, until margarine melts. Stir to mix.

2. Add cereal, dried apple and banana slices, and wheat germ. Toss gently to combine.

3. Bake 12 to 15 minutes, stirring frequently, until crispy. Let cool completely, then store in an airtight container for up to 3 days.

PER SERVING   Calories 130   Total Fat 2 g   Saturated Fat <1 g
Cholesterol 0 mg   Percentage calories from fat 11%

Slimming Soups and Salads

Because soups and salads are so often paired together for lunch or a light supper, I've grouped them in this chapter, though there is no requirement that they appear in the same meal. In general, both these types of foods tend to be lower in calories as well as in fat, so they are good choices for dieters. They also have a lighter feel in the stomach, so they are popular with active people. I love homemade soups on a chilly day, and it may surprise you how many there are that can be whipped up from almost scratch in no time at all. And salads are great especially in summer, when you don't feel like turning on the stove.

This chapter will also give you a broad range of salads, from heartier main-course salads, such as Tortellini and Shrimp Salad and Crunchy Chicken Salad, to lighter fare and side salads to accompany a meal, such as Lemon Caesar Salad.

My personal favorite answer to any meal is soup; it has saved the day for me many times. I find heartier soups, such as Ravioli Watercress Soup and Cheesy Chili Bean Soup, are perfect solutions to everything from mid-winter blues to frantic weekday dinners. For starters, a lighter soup like Creamy Fresh Tomato Soup or Spicy Crab Gazpacho fits the bill.

With both soups and salads, reduced- and low-fat cheeses, nonfat yogurt and sour cream, beans, and other healthful complex carbohydrates keep the proportion of calories from fat under 30 percent. And all are designed to move from kitchen to table in nothing flat.

Cream of Asparagus and Mushroom Soup

Makes 4 servings

In this low-fat soup, richness is achieved by using skim milk instead of cream and a reduced-fat canned soup as a base. Fresh asparagus adds a note of spring green to an otherwise instant preparation.

1 pound fresh asparagus, cut into 2-inch lengths

1 (0-ounce) can sliced mushrooms, drained

1 (10¾-ounce) can condensed reduced-fat cream of mushroom soup

1 cup reduced-sodium chicken broth

½ cup skim milk

1 tablespoon fresh lemon juice

½ teaspoon dried tarragon

¼ teaspoon salt

⅛ teaspoon ground white pepper

1½ teaspoons prepared white horseradish

1. In a large saucepan of boiling salted water, cook asparagus until just tender, about 3 minutes. Drain and rinse briefly under cold running water.

2. Transfer asparagus to a food processor. Add mushrooms and process until finely chopped. Add canned soup, chicken broth, milk, lemon juice, tarragon, salt, and pepper. Puree until smooth and creamy.

3. Transfer soup to a large saucepan. Cook about 5 minutes over medium heat, until heated through.

4. Stir in horseradish. Cook 2 minutes longer to blend flavors.

PER SERVING   Calories 83   Total Fat 2 g   Saturated Fat 1 g
Cholesterol 7 mg   Percentage calories from fat 22%

Cheesy Chili Bean Soup

Makes 8 servings

2 teaspoons reduced-calorie margarine

2 medium celery ribs, chopped

½ cup chopped scallions

2 garlic cloves, minced

1 (28-ounce) can pasta-ready tomatoes

1 cup reduced-sodium chicken broth

1 tablespoon chili powder

2 teaspoons balsamic vinegar

1½ cups drained canned black beans

1 cup drained canned red kidney beans

1 can drained canned chickpeas

¼ cup shredded reduced-fat Cheddar cheese

¼ cup shredded reduced-fat Monterey Jack cheese

1. Melt margarine in a large Dutch oven. Add celery, scallions, and garlic. Cook over medium heat, stirring occasionally, until celery is tender, 4 to 5 minutes. Stir in tomatoes, broth, chili powder, vinegar, and 4 cups water. Bring to a boil.

2. Reduce heat to low. Stir in black beans, kidney beans, and chickpeas. Simmer 10 minutes.

3. To serve, ladle hot soup into bowls and top each portion with equal amounts of shredded cheeses.

PER SERVING   Calories 156   Total Fat 3 g   Saturated Fat 1 g
Cholesterol 5 mg   Percentage calories from fat 16%

Chicken Barley Soup

Makes 4 servings

Quick-cooking barley is widely available and is a great time-saver. Check your grocery section right next to the regular barley to find it.

2 skinless boneless chicken breast halves (4½ to 5 ounces each)

2 (12¾-ounce) cans reduced-sodium chicken broth

2 teaspoons olive oil

1 cup chopped fresh fennel or celery

½ cup chopped onion

½ cup chopped carrots

½ cup quick-cooking barley

½ teaspoon dried thyme

1 bay leaf

1 cup finely chopped fresh spinach (use prewashed to save time)
          or 1 cup thawed frozen chopped spinach

Salt and freshly ground black pepper

1. Place chicken breasts in a medium saucepan. Add chicken broth and ½ cup water. Bring to a simmer, reduce heat to medium-low, and cook 12 to 15 minutes, or until chicken is just white throughout. Remove chicken to a plate and let cool. Strain broth into a bowl and set aside.

2. In a large saucepan, heat oil over medium-high heat. Stir in fennel, onion, and carrots and cook 1 minute. Stir in barley and thyme. Add reserved broth, ½ cup water, and bay leaf. Bring to a boil, reduce heat to low, partially cover, and simmer 10 to 12 minutes, until barley is tender.

3. Meanwhile, tear chicken breasts into shreds. When barley is tender, stir in chicken and spinach. Simmer 2 minutes longer, until chicken and spinach are hot. Remove bay leaf and season with salt and pepper to taste before serving.

PER SERVING Calories 205 Total Fat 3 g Saturated Fat <1 g
Cholesterol 41 mg Percentage calories from fat 16%

Bacon and Chickpea Soup

Makes 4 servings

1 (15-ounce) can chickpeas, rinsed and drained
¾ cup evaporated skimmed milk
⅓ cup chicken broth
1 teaspoon olive oil
½ cup chopped scallions
2 strips turkey bacon, cut into ½-inch dice
2 garlic cloves, minced
½ teaspoon dried oregano
2 teaspoons balsamic vinegar
¼ teaspoon salt
1 medium tomato, chopped

1. In a food processor, combine chickpeas, evaporated milk, and broth. Puree until smooth. Set chickpea puree aside.

2. In a large saucepan, heat oil over medium heat. Add scallions, bacon, garlic, and oregano. Cook, stirring frequently, until bacon is lightly browned, 4 to 5 minutes.

3. Stir in chickpea puree, vinegar, and salt. Simmer 10 minutes. Serve hot, garnished with chopped tomato.

PER SERVING Calories 148 Total Fat 4 g Saturated Fat 1 g
Cholesterol 7 mg Percentage calories from fat 25%

Spicy Crab Gazpacho

Makes 4 servings

*P*acked with summer fresh vegetables, this soup is the perfect solution on hot and steamy days when the last thing you want to do is face the kitchen.

¼ cup flat-leaf parsley sprigs

3 garlic cloves, crushed

3 cups spicy mixed vegetable juice

6 large ripe tomatoes (about 3 pounds), seeded and quartered

2 medium cucumbers, peeled, seeded, and coarsely chopped

3 celery ribs, quartered

1 medium red onion, quartered

2 tablespoons red wine vinegar

½ teaspoon salt

¼ teaspoon hot red pepper sauce

¼ cup nonfat plain yogurt

1 teaspoon grated lime zest

¼ teaspoon ground cumin

½ pound imitation or fresh crabmeat, shredded

1. In a food processor, combine parsley and garlic with half of vegetable juice. Process until parsley and garlic are minced. Add half of tomatoes, cucumbers, celery, and onion. Pulse until vegetables are coarsely chopped; do not puree. Transfer to a large soup tureen.

2. Add remaining vegetable juice, tomatoes, cucumbers, celery, onion, and the vinegar and salt to food processor; process until coarsely chopped. Add to tureen. Stir in hot sauce. If you have the time, cover and refrigerate until ice cold.

3. In a small bowl, blend yogurt with lime zest and cumin. To serve, ladle soup into 4 bowls. Top each with equal amounts of crabmeat and a dollop of seasoned yogurt.

PER SERVING   Calories 178   Total Fat 2 g   Saturated Fat <1 g
Cholesterol 9 mg   Percentage calories from fat 9%

Ravioli Watercress Soup

Makes 4 servings

This is a soup the whole family will love to see appear at the dinner table. Fresh ravioli is a real time-saver in the cooking department. I used cheese ravioli but meat-filled can certainly be used instead.

1 (14½-ounce) can reduced-sodium chicken broth
½ cup tomato juice
2½ cups mini fresh cheese ravioli
½ teaspoon dried basil
¼ teaspoon dried oregano
¼ teaspoon crushed fennel seeds
1½ cups coarsely chopped watercress
¼ teaspoon salt
1 to 2 drops hot pepper sauce
2 tablespoons grated Parmesan cheese

1. In a large saucepan, combine broth, tomato juice, and ¾ cup water. Bring to a boil over medium-high heat. Stir in ravioli, basil, oregano, and fennel seeds. Boil, stirring frequently, 5 to 7 minutes, until ravioli are tender.

2. Stir in watercress, salt, and hot sauce. Cook until watercress wilts, 1 to 2 minutes longer.

3. To serve, ladle hot soup into 4 bowls. Top each with 1½ teaspoons grated cheese.

PER SERVING   Calories 202   Total Fat 5 g   Saturated Fat 2 g
Cholesterol 21 mg   Percentage calories from fat 21%

Creamy Fresh Tomato Soup

Makes 4 servings

*T*hrow *away that can opener. Here's a homemade soup, prepared from fresh, summer-ripe tomatoes, that's ready in minutes. If you want to make the same soup in the middle of winter, substitute a 28-ounce can of peeled plum tomatoes, drained and chopped.*

½ cup chopped scallions

1 teaspoon olive oil

3 large ripe tomatoes (about 2¼ pounds), cut into 1-inch chunks

½ cup fresh basil leaves

⅔ cup skim milk

½ cup mixed vegetable juice

1 tablespoon fresh lemon juice

¼ teaspoon salt

¼ teaspoon freshly ground black pepper

1. In a large nonreactive saucepan, cook scallions in oil over medium heat, stirring frequently, until wilted, about 2 minutes. Add tomatoes, raise heat to medium-high, and cook, stirring often, until they are softened and begin to give up their juices, about 5 minutes.

2. Transfer to a food processor. Add basil and puree until smooth. Return soup to saucepan.

3. Stir in milk, vegetable juice, lemon juice, salt, and pepper. Simmer until heated through, about 5 minutes.

PER SERVING   Calories 74   Total Fat 2 g   Saturated Fat 0 g
Cholesterol 1 mg   Percentage calories from fat 19%

Chilled Summer Fruit Soup

Makes 4 servings

Fruit soups are perfect for summer luncheons, where something refreshing is always wanted. Ripeness is paramount here, since the flavor of the fresh fruit forms the base of the soup.

4 ripe peaches, peeled and quartered

4 ripe nectarines, peeled and quartered

1 pint strawberries, hulled and cut in half

1½ cups skim milk

1 cup crushed ice

½ cup plus 2 tablespoons nonfat sour cream

1 tablespoon honey

½ teaspoon ground ginger

Pinch cinnamon

2 tablespoons chopped fresh mint (optional)

1. In a food processor, combine peaches, nectarines, strawberries, 1 cup of the milk, and the ice. Process until smooth.

2. Add sour cream, honey, ginger, cinnamon, and remaining milk. Process until blended and smooth. If you have time, transfer to a covered container and refrigerate until chilled.

3. To serve, ladle soup into 4 bowls. Garnish each with 1½ teaspoons chopped mint.

PER SERVING   Calories 220   Total Fat 1 g   Saturated Fat 0 g
Cholesterol 2 mg   Percentage calories from fat 5%

Crunchy Chicken Salad

Makes 4 servings

This salad has a definite oriental taste. As always to save time, use the shredding disk of your food processor to prepare the vegetables. Already shredded cabbage is available in many supermarket produce departments. If you want a more substantial dish, toss in crispy Chinese noodles just before serving.

½ cup vegetable or chicken broth

¼ cup rice wine vinegar

1 tablespoon soy sauce

1 tablespoon grated fresh ginger

1½ teaspoons Asian sesame oil

¼ teaspoon salt

¼ teaspoon crushed hot red pepper

2 cups shredded red cabbage

¾ pound cooked chicken breast, torn into large shreds

1 cup shredded green cabbage or celery

½ cup fresh bean sprouts

½ cup shredded carrots

2 tablespoons chopped fresh cilantro (optional)

1. In a small bowl, whisk together broth, vinegar, soy sauce, ginger, sesame oil, salt, and hot pepper until well blended.

2. In a large bowl, combine red cabbage, chicken, green cabbage, bean sprouts, and carrots. Add dressing and toss to mix well. Garnish with cilantro, if desired.

PER SERVING   Calories 138   Total Fat 3 g   Saturated Fat <1 g
Cholesterol 49 mg   Percentage calories from fat 19%

Lamb and Potato Salad

Makes 4 servings

*T*his main-course salad makes an instant lunch or light supper whenever you have leftover lamb on hand. If you have leftover cooked potatoes, by all means, use those and save yourself even more time.

1 pound small red potatoes, scrubbed

¼ cup balsamic vinegar

2 tablespoons broth or water

2 teaspoons olive oil

2 teaspoons capers, minced

1 garlic clove, crushed through a press

1 teaspoon dried oregano

¼ teaspoon salt

¼ teaspoon freshly ground black pepper

4 cups packed coarsely chopped romaine lettuce

¾ pound cooked lean lamb, trimmed of fat and thinly sliced

½ cup chopped tomatoes

2 tablespoons crumbled herb-flavored feta cheese

1. Halve or quarter potatoes, depending on size. In a large saucepan of boiling salted water, cook potatoes until tender, 10 to 15 minutes. Drain into a colander and rinse under cold running water to cool.

2. In a large salad bowl, whisk together vinegar, broth, oil, capers, garlic, oregano, salt, and pepper until blended. Add potatoes, lettuce, lamb, tomatoes, and cheese. Toss to mix well. Serve at room temperature.

PER SERVING   Calories 237   Total Fat 8 g   Saturated Fat 3 g
Cholesterol 44 mg   Percentage calories from fat 30%

Tortellini and Shrimp Salad

Makes 8 servings

*C*onsider *this salad for your next picnic or barbecue. It makes a welcome change from the usual cold fare. The servings indicated above are as a starter or side salad; it will serve 4 to 6 as a main course. The recipe doubles easily.*

1 (9-ounce) package fresh cheese tortellini
½ cup nonfat vinaigrette dressing
2 tablespoons minced scallions
1 tablespoon grated Parmesan cheese
¼ teaspoon salt
¼ teaspoon freshly ground black pepper
¾ pound cooked peeled medium shrimp
1 medium red bell pepper, cut into strips
1 cup cherry tomato halves
½ cup chopped celery
¼ cup shredded fresh basil
Lemon wedges

1. In a large pot of boiling salted water, cook tortellini until tender but still firm, about 5 minutes. Drain and rinse briefly under cold running water; drain well.

2. Meanwhile, in a large bowl, whisk together vinaigrette, scallions, cheese, salt, and black pepper. Add tortellini, shrimp, bell pepper, tomatoes, celery, and basil. Toss to mix well.

3. Serve at once or chill. Serve with lemon wedges to squeeze over salad.

PER SERVING   Calories 162   Total Fat 3 g   Saturated Fat 1 g
Cholesterol 78 mg   Percentage calories from fat 18%

Oriental Steak Salad with
Red Onion and Mandarin Oranges

Makes 4 servings

*S*weet *onion and oranges present a lovely counterpoint here to the tart-salty teriyaki dressing. If you have leftover steak of any kind, by all means, use it in place of the flank steak.*

    ¾ pound trimmed lean flank steak

    1 tablespoon sesame seeds

    3 cups packed torn red leaf lettuce

    1½ cups packed torn Boston lettuce

    1 medium red onion, thinly sliced and separated into rings

    1 cup unsweetened mandarin orange slices

    1 tablespoon teriyaki sauce

    1 tablespoon lime juice

    2 teaspoons hoisin sauce

    ¼ cup nonfat plain yogurt

    2 tablespoons orange juice

    1 tablespoon honey

    2 teaspoons Dijon mustard

    ¼ teaspoon ground ginger

    1. Preheat broiler or gas grill. Broil steak about 4 inches from heat or grill over high heat, turning once, until rare, 3 to 5 minutes per side, or longer to desired doneness. Let stand 10 minutes. Trim off any visible fat and carve against grain into thin slices.

2. Meanwhile, in a small dry skillet, cook sesame seeds over medium heat, shaking pan often, until seeds are fragrant and lightly toasted, about 3 minutes.

3. In a large bowl, combine steak, red leaf lettuce, Boston lettuce, onion, and orange slices. Toss to mix. In a small bowl, whisk together teriyaki sauce, lime juice, and hoisin sauce until well blended. Pour over salad and toss to mix.

4. In another small bowl, whisk together yogurt, orange juice, honey, mustard, and ginger until well blended. To serve, divide salad evenly among 4 plates. Top each with a large dollop of yogurt topping and ¾ teaspoon toasted sesame seeds.

PER SERVING   Calories 206   Total Fat 6 g   Saturated Fat 2 g
Cholesterol 31 mg   Percentage calories from fat 27%

Lemon Caesar Salad

Classic Caesar salads are laden with fat and cholesterol. This version omits the traditional raw egg in the dressing and ups the lemon juice for a refreshing, tangy taste. It makes a great starter or side salad. To serve as a main dish, top with grilled chicken or fish.

¼ cup dry-pack sun-dried tomato bits

4 slices Italian bread, cut ½ inch thick

4 garlic cloves

1½ teaspoons grainy Dijon mustard

1 teaspoon anchovy paste

1 teaspoon Worcestershire sauce

¼ teaspoon freshly ground black pepper

¼ cup fresh lemon juice

¼ cup chicken broth

1½ teaspoons olive oil

8 cups packed torn romaine lettuce

2 tablespoons grated Parmesan cheese

1. Place dried tomato bits in a small bowl, cover with hot water, and let stand about 10 minutes, until softened. Drain well.

2. Meanwhile, toast bread in toaster or under broiler. Cut 1 garlic clove in half and rub over bread. Cut bread into ¾-inch cubes. Set garlic croutons aside.

3. Crush remaining 3 garlic cloves through a press into a large salad bowl. Whisk in mustard, anchovy paste, Worcestershire, pepper, lemon juice, broth, and oil.

4. Add lettuce to bowl and toss to coat with dressing. Sprinkle dried tomato bits, Parmesan cheese, and garlic croutons over salad. Toss lightly to mix. Serve at once.

PER SERVING   Calories 102   Total Fat 3 g   Saturated Fat 1 g
Cholesterol 3 mg   Percentage calories from fat 29%

Watercress Salad with Feta Cheese, Bacon Dressing, and Garlic Toasts

Makes 4 servings

2 strips turkey bacon

6 ounces Italian bread, sliced ½ inch thick

2 garlic cloves, 1 halved, 1 minced

2 tablespoons balsamic vinegar

2 tablespoons chicken broth or water

1 teaspoon olive oil

2 teaspoons grainy Dijon mustard

½ teaspoon oregano

1½ cups trimmed watercress

1 cup packed torn red leaf lettuce

3 tablespoons feta cheese, preferably pepper-flavored

1. Place bacon between several layers of microwave-safe paper towels. Microwave on high 2 to 4 minutes, until crisp. Crumble bacon.

2. Toast bread in toaster or under broiler. Rub one side of each bread slice with cut sides of halved garlic.

3. In a small bowl, whisk together vinegar, chicken broth, oil, mustard, minced garlic, and oregano until combined. Stir bacon into dressing.

4. In a salad bowl, combine watercress and leaf lettuce. Add dressing and toss to mix well. Divide salad among 4 plates. Sprinkle feta cheese on top and serve with garlic toasts.

PER SERVING   Calories 169   Total Fat 5 g   Saturated Fat 2 g
Cholesterol 11 mg   Percentage calories from fat 28%

Pasta Presto

Who could have imagined just a few decades ago that the word *pasta* would so frequently be on the lips of food lovers everywhere. Its boundaries are seemingly limitless, and its popularity seems to exceed that of any other food. Since it is naturally low in fat and cooks up in roughly 10 minutes, pasta is a natural when you want to produce food that is *Low Fat in Nothing Flat.*

I enjoy taking advantage of all the different pasta shapes, which range from thin capellini to chubby orechiette ("little ears") to tubular noodles, like ziti. While any brand will do, I recommend a good imported pasta made with durum wheat, which will cook up *al dente,* tender but still firm, with a little resistance when you bite into it.

Speedy sauces are easy to prepare while the pasta cooks. Toppings have moved way beyond plain tomato sauce to quickly sautéed vegetables, seafood, and poultry—with even a number of uncooked sauces thrown in for good measure.

Fast, fresh, and nutritionally sound are three key terms to associate with pasta. The versatility, nutritional makeup, and ease of preparation of pasta fit in perfectly with what this book is all about. By stocking up on a few basics, you can come home any night and have a delicious nutritionally sound meal ready within minutes. For dieters, pasta topped with a lean sauce can provide a meal packed with complex carbohydrates and low in fat.

This chapter celebrates pasta in all its many different guises: curly, long, straight, wide, or thin, dried and fresh. You'll find quick versions of classic dishes, like Spaghettini with Red Clam Sauce and Broiled Macaroni and Cheese, as well as inventive ideas like Bow Ties with Bacon and Bread Crumbs and Creamy Dijon Noodles with Mushrooms and Spinach. All use natural and new low-fat ingredients and products to give you maximum flavor with minimum fat. And all this wonderful pasta can be made ready as soon as you say "Presto."

Bow Ties with Bacon and Bread Crumbs

Makes 4 servings

If you have any stale French or Italian bread, by all means use it for the bread crumbs. Just cut thick slices and toss them into the food processor. Another time-saver is the prepared fresh broccoli florets that many supermarkets now sell.

12 ounces bow tie pasta

4 cups broccoli florets

12 dry-pack sun-dried tomato halves, cut into 3 or 4 pieces each

½ cup boiling water

2 teaspoons olive oil

2 slices turkey bacon, cut into ½-inch pieces

8 ounces dry bread crumbs

3 garlic cloves, minced

2 teaspoons balsamic vinegar

¼ teaspoon salt

2 tablespoons grated Parmesan cheese

1. In a large pot of boiling salted water, cook pasta 5 minutes. Add broccoli and cook until pasta is tender but still firm and broccoli is crisp-tender, 5 to 7 minutes longer. Drain into a colander and rinse briefly under cold running water. Drain well.

2. Meanwhile, place dried tomatoes in a small heatproof bowl. Pour on boiling water and let stand 5 to 10 minutes to soften.

3. In a large nonstick skillet, heat oil over medium-high heat. Add bacon and cook, stirring often, until crisp, about 2 minutes. Remove with a slotted spoon and set aside.

4. Add bread crumbs to skillet and cook, stirring often, until golden, 2 to 4 minutes. Remove with slotted spoon and set aside. Add garlic to skillet and cook, stirring constantly, 1 minute. Pour tomatoes with their water into skillet; return bacon to pan. Bring to a boil and cook until liquid is reduced by half, about 2 minutes. Stir in vinegar and salt and cook 1 minute longer.

5. Add pasta and broccoli to skillet. Toss over medium-high heat to warm through and mix well. Sprinkle toasted crumbs and cheese on top just before serving.

PER SERVING   Calories 585   Total Fat 8 g   Saturated Fat 2 g
Cholesterol 7 mg   Percentage calories from fat 12%

Green and White Angel Hair

Makes 4 servings

Because angel hair pasta is so thin, it is a great time-saver. The fresh variety, found in the refrigerated section of many supermarkets, is ready in just a minute or two.

2 teaspoons olive oil

3 garlic cloves, minced

¾ cup reduced-sodium chicken broth

3 tablespoons fresh lemon juice

¼ cup chopped fresh basil

½ teaspoon dried thyme

¼ teaspoon salt

½ cup chopped roasted red peppers (½ a 7-ounce jar)

1 large plum tomato, seeded and chopped

6 ounces fresh spinach angel hair pasta

6 ounces fresh plain angel hair pasta

1. In a large nonstick skillet, heat oil over medium heat. Add garlic and cook, stirring often, 1 minute. Stir in chicken broth and lemon juice. Bring to a boil; reduce heat to low. Stir in basil, thyme, and salt. Simmer 2 minutes. Stir in roasted peppers and tomato. Simmer over low heat 3 minutes to blend flavors.

2. Meanwhile, in a large pot of boiling salted water, cook both types of pasta together 1 to 2 minutes, until just tender. Drain and transfer to a serving bowl. Pour sauce over pasta, toss gently to coat, and serve at once.

PER SERVING   Calories 291   Total Fat 4 g   Saturated Fat 1 g
Cholesterol 63 mg   Percentage calories from fat 13%

Bucatini with Lemon Shrimp

Makes 4 servings

This fresh-from-the-sea entree is full of cool summer flavors. Prepare when the temperature is soaring and the last thing you want to do is stand over a hot stove.

12 ounces bucatini or spaghetti
1 pound cooked peeled medium shrimp
½ cup thawed frozen peas
½ cup chopped fresh basil
¼ cup chopped flat-leaf parsley
3 tablespoons fresh lemon juice
2 garlic cloves, minced
2 teaspoons olive oil
½ teaspoon salt-free lemon-herb seasoning blend
1 tablespoon grated Parmesan cheese

1. In a large pot of boiling water, cook bucatini 10 to 12 minutes, until tender but still firm. Add shrimp and cook 30 seconds to heat through.

2. Meanwhile, in a large serving bowl, combine peas, basil, parsley, lemon juice, garlic, olive oil, and lemon-herb seasoning. Toss to mix well.

3. Drain pasta and shrimp and add to bowl. Toss to mix well. Sprinkle Parmesan cheese on top and serve at once.

PER SERVING   Calories 488   Total Fat 6 g   Saturated Fat 1 g
Cholesterol 174 mg   Percentage calories from fat 11%

Capellini with Spicy Arugula

Makes 4 servings

Arugula, with its wonderful peppery flavor, adds a lot of flavor without fat and calories. Once rinsed, it's practically ready to use; just trim off the tough stem ends.

1 tablespoon olive oil

1 medium red onion, chopped

2 garlic cloves, minced

½ teaspoon crushed hot red pepper

1 (28-ounce) can plum tomatoes, drained and chopped

¾ cup coarsely chopped marinated artichoke hearts

2 teaspoons balsamic vinegar

12 ounces capellini

2 bunches arugula, coarsely chopped

½ cup shredded nonfat mozzarella cheese

1. In a large nonstick skillet, heat oil over medium-high heat. Add red onion, garlic, and hot pepper. Cook, stirring often, 3 to 4 minutes, until onion is softened. Add tomatoes and artichokes. Bring to a boil, reduce heat to medium-low, and simmer 6 to 8 minutes, until sauce thickens slightly. Stir in vinegar and cook 1 minute longer.

2. Meanwhile, in a large pot of boiling salted water, cook capellini 6 to 8 minutes, until tender but still firm.

3. Place arugula in a large serving bowl. Drain capellini and add to bowl. Pour tomato sauce over pasta and toss to mix well. Sprinkle mozzarella cheese on top and serve at once.

PER SERVING   Calories 464   Total Fat 9 g   Saturated Fat 1 g
Cholesterol 3 mg   Percentage calories from fat 17%

Fusilli with Eggplant and Scallops

Makes 4 servings

12 ounces fusilli

1 tablespoon olive oil

1 medium onion, chopped

2 celery ribs, chopped

2 garlic cloves, minced

1 large eggplant (1 pound), cut into ¾-inch dice

2 large tomatoes, chopped, or 1 (14½-ounce) can diced
      tomatoes, drained

½ teaspoon fennel seeds, crushed

10 ounces bay scallops

¼ cup chopped flat-leaf parsley

1. In a large pot of boiling salted water, cook fusilli until tender but still firm, 10 to 12 minutes. Drain.

2. Meanwhile, in a large nonstick skillet, heat oil over medium heat. Add onion, celery, and garlic. Cook, stirring often, 2 to 3 minutes, until tender. Add eggplant and cook, stirring often, 5 minutes. Stir in tomatoes and fennel seeds and cook, stirring often, 5 minutes longer, or until eggplant is tender.

3. Add scallops and cook until scallops are firm and opaque throughout, 3 to 4 minutes.

4. Transfer pasta to a large serving bowl. Top with scallop sauce and toss gently. Sprinkle parsley on top and serve.

PER SERVING   Calories 474   Total Fat 6 g   Saturated Fat 1 g
Cholesterol 23 mg   Percentage calories from fat 11%

Creamy Fettuccine with Peas

Makes 4 servings

12 ounces fettuccine

1½ cups skim milk

2 garlic cloves, minced

1 tablespoon all-purpose flour

½ teaspoon salt-free garlic-herb seasoning blend or ¼ teaspoon
garlic powder

3 tablespoons nonfat cream cheese

1 (10-ounce) box frozen peas, thawed

½ cup grated Romano cheese

2 tablespoons butter-flavored sprinkles

¼ teaspoon salt

¼ teaspoon freshly ground black pepper

1. In a large pot of boiling salted water, cook fettuccine 10 to 12 minutes, until tender but still firm.

2. Meanwhile, in a medium saucepan, bring milk and garlic to a boil over medium heat. Gradually whisk in flour and herb seasoning. Cook, whisking constantly, until thickened and smooth, 2 to 3 minutes.

3. Add cream cheese and cook, stirring, 1 minute or until melted. Stir in peas, Romano cheese, butter sprinkles, salt, and pepper. Cook 2 minutes longer, or until heated through and smooth.

4. Drain pasta and place in a large bowl. Pour sauce over pasta and toss to coat. Serve at once.

PER SERVING   Calories 494   Total Fat 8 g   Saturated Fat 1 g
Cholesterol 99 mg   Percentage calories from fat 14%

Linguine with Roasted Pepper Cream Sauce

Makes 4 servings

12 ounces spinach linguine

1 (7-ounce) jar roasted red peppers, drained

¾ cup nonfat ricotta cheese

2 tablespoons tomato sauce

2 tablespoons grated Parmesan cheese

½ teaspoon garlic powder

1 teaspoon olive oil

1 cup chopped scallions

½ cup skim milk

¼ cup chopped flat-leaf parsley

1. In a large pot of boiling salted water, cook linguine 10 to 12 minutes, until tender but still firm.

2. Meanwhile, in a food processor, combine roasted peppers, ricotta, tomato sauce, Parmesan cheese, and garlic powder. Puree until smooth.

3. In a medium saucepan, heat oil over medium heat. Add scallions and cook, stirring often, 2 to 3 minutes, until wilted. Stir in milk and roasted pepper puree. Cook, stirring constantly, 2 to 3 minutes, until heated through.

4. To serve, drain pasta and place in a large bowl. Pour sauce over pasta and toss to mix well. Sprinkle with parsley and serve at once.

PER SERVING Calories 417 Total Fat 3 g Saturated Fat 1 g
Cholesterol 3 mg Percentage calories from fat 7%

Linguine with Mixed Herb Pesto

Makes 4 servings

Traditional pesto is made simply with fresh basil, olive oil, garlic, pine nuts, and Parmesan cheese. Here defatted chicken broth replaces most of the oil.

12 ounces plain or spinach linguine

1 tablespoon pine nuts

1 cup loosely packed fresh basil leaves

1 cup loosely packed flat-leaf parsley sprigs

¼ cup fresh mint leaves or 1 teaspoon dried

2 tablespoons grated Parmesan cheese

1½ teaspoons grated lemon zest

2 garlic cloves

1¼ cups fat-free reduced-sodium chicken broth

2 teaspoons olive oil

½ teaspoon salt

¼ teaspoon freshly ground black pepper

1. In a large pot of boiling salted water, cook linguine 10 to 12 minutes, until tender but still firm.

2. Meanwhile, in a small dry skillet, cook pine nuts over medium-high heat, shaking pan constantly, until golden brown, 2 to 3 minutes.

3. In a food processor, chop basil, parsley, mint, Parmesan cheese, lemon zest, pine nuts, and garlic. With machine on, slowly add broth, olive oil, salt, and pepper. Process until pesto is smooth.

4. Drain linguine and place in a large serving bowl. Top with pesto, toss to mix well, and serve.

PER SERVING   Calories 388   Total Fat 6 g   Saturated Fat 1 g
Cholesterol 2 mg   Percentage calories from fat 13%

Gorgonzola Rigatoni

Makes 6 servings

12 ounces rigatoni

1 tablespoon reduced-calorie margarine

3 tablespoons all-purpose flour

2 cups warm skim milk

¼ teaspoon nutmeg

Pinch ground white pepper

1 (10-ounce) box frozen artichoke hearts, thawed and chopped

2 ounces gorgonzola cheese, crumbled (about ½ cup)

1 tablespoon grated provolone cheese

1 tablespoon seasoned dry bread crumbs

1. Preheat broiler. Spray a large shallow casserole with nonstick cooking spray. In a large port of boiling salted water, cook rigatoni until tender but still firm, 10 to 12 minutes.

2. In a large saucepan, melt margarine over medium heat. Stir in flour. Gradually whisk in milk, nutmeg, and pepper until blended. Cook, whisking constantly, until sauce boils and thickens, 4 to 5 minutes.

3. Drain pasta and pour into prepared casserole. Add sauce, artichokes, gorgonzola, and provolone cheese. Toss gently to blend.

4. Sprinkle crumbs on top. Broil about 6 inches from heat 2 to 4 minutes, until golden brown and bubbly.

PER SERVING   Calories 323   Total Fat 6 g   Saturated Fat 3 g
Cholesterol 11 mg   Percentage calories from fat 16%

Linguine with Sausage and Spinach

Makes 4 servings

¼ cup golden raisins
½ cup boiling water
12 ounces linguine
1 tablespoon olive oil
1 medium red onion, chopped
2 garlic cloves, minced
8 ounces sweet or hot Italian turkey sausage, casings removed
½ cup beef broth
1 pound recipe-ready fresh spinach leaves, cut into thin strips
Freshly ground black pepper

1. Place raisins in a small heatproof bowl. Pour boiling water over raisins and set aside to plump, 10 to 15 minutes. Drain when soft.

2. Meanwhile, in a large pot of boiling salted water, cook pasta until tender but still firm, 10 to 12 minutes.

3. While pasta is cooking, in a large nonstick skillet, heat oil over medium heat. Add red onion and garlic and cook, stirring often, until tender, 2 to 3 minutes. Add sausage and cook, stirring to break meat into small pieces, until no longer pink, 5 to 7 minutes.

4. Pour in broth; bring to a boil. Stir in spinach. Cover skillet and cook 1 to 2 minutes longer, until spinach wilts.

5. Drain pasta and place in a large serving bowl. Add sausage-spinach mixture and drained raisins. Toss to mix well. Sprinkle with pepper to taste.

PER SERVING   Calories 507   Total Fat 11 g   Saturated Fat 2 g
Cholesterol 30 mg   Percentage calories from fat 20%

Broiled Macaroni and Cheese

Makes 4 servings

10 ounces elbow macaroni

1 tablespoon reduced-calorie margarine

1 cup chopped scallions

¼ cup all-purpose flour

2½ cups hot skim milk

1 tablespoon Dijon mustard

1½ cups shredded low-fat Cheddar cheese

1 tablespoon grated Parmesan cheese

1 medium tomato, chopped

½ teaspoon paprika

½ teaspoon salt

¼ teaspoon freshly ground black pepper

1 tablespoon seasoned dry bread crumbs

1. Preheat broiler. Spray an 11 by 7-inch baking dish with nonstick cooking spray. In a large pot of boiling salted water, cook macaroni 10 to 12 minutes, until tender but still firm; drain.

2. Meanwhile, in a medium saucepan, melt margarine over medium heat. Add scallions and cook, stirring often, 2 to 3 minutes, until wilted. Stir in flour and cook 1 minute. Gradually whisk in hot milk and mustard. Boil, stirring, 2 to 3 minutes, until thick. Reduce heat to low and stir in Cheddar cheese, Parmesan cheese, tomatoes, paprika, salt, and pepper.

3. Place macaroni in baking dish. Add cheese sauce and toss to mix well. Sprinkle bread crumbs on top. Broil 4 to 5 minutes, until golden and bubbly.

PER SERVING   Calories 514   Total Fat 11 g   Saturated Fat 6 g
Cholesterol 34 mg   Percentage calories from fat 20%

Creamy Dijon Noodles with Mushrooms and Spinach

Makes 4 servings

For a low-cholesterol as well as low-fat dish, this recipe is made with no-yolk noodles. Use wide noodles in order to catch all this delicious sauce. To save time, look for sliced fresh mushrooms packaged in the produce section of your supermarket

½ cup golden raisins

12 ounces wide no-yolk noodles

2 teaspoons olive oil

1 medium onion, chopped

1 pound mushrooms, thinly sliced

1 cup reduced-sodium beef broth

2 tablespoons white wine vinegar

1½ tablespoons grainy Dijon mustard

½ teaspoon salt

1 tablespoon cornstarch

1 cup thawed frozen chopped spinach, squeezed dry

1. Place raisins in a small heatproof bowl and cover with boiling water. Set aside until softened, about 10 minutes. Drain, reserving 2 tablespoons water.

2. Meanwhile, in a large pot of boiling salted water, cook noodles 8 to 10 minutes, until tender but still firm.

3. While noodles are cooking, heat oil in large nonstick skillet over medium-high heat. Add onion and cook 2 minutes to soften slightly. Add mushrooms and cook, stirring often, 3 to 4 minutes, until mushrooms are tender.

4. In a small bowl, whisk together broth, vinegar, reserved raisin water, mustard, salt, and cornstarch until cornstarch is dissolved. Stir into skillet and bring to a boil. Add raisins and cook 1 minute, stirring, until sauce thickens. Add spinach and cook 1 to 2 minutes, until heated through.

5. Drain noodles and place in a large serving bowl. Add mushroom-spinach sauce and toss to mix well. Serve at once.

PER SERVING   Calories 434   Total Fat 5 g   Saturated Fat 1 g
Cholesterol 0 mg   Percentage calories from fat 9%

Chinese Beef and Noodle Stir-Fry

Makes 4 servings

1 tablespoon teriyaki sauce

1 tablespoon chicken broth or water

2 teaspoons brown sugar

1 garlic clove, crushed

¼ teaspoon ground ginger

6 ounces trimmed lean sirloin steak, thinly sliced

10 ounces Chinese egg noodles or thin egg noodles

2 teaspoons peanut oil

1 cup scallion pieces (1-inch)

1 red bell pepper, cut into thin strips

½ teaspoon Asian sesame oil

Crushed hot red pepper

1. In a large bowl, combine teriyaki sauce, chicken broth, brown sugar, garlic, and ginger. Add steak; toss to coat well. In a large pot of boiling salted water, cook noodles until tender but still firm, 4 to 6 minutes; drain.

2. In a large wok or nonstick skillet, heat 1 teaspoon peanut oil over medium-high heat. With a slotted spoon, remove steak from marinade and add to skillet. Stir-fry 2 to 3 minutes, until no longer pink. Add any marinade left in bowl and cook 1 minute longer. Remove steak from wok.

3. Heat remaining 1 teaspoon peanut oil in wok over medium-high heat. Add noodles and stir-fry 2 to 3 minutes, until crisp. Add scallions and pepper strips. Stir-fry 2 minutes. Add steak and cook 1 minute or until heated through. Drizzle with sesame oil, season with hot pepper to taste and serve.

PER SERVING   Calories 377   Total Fat 8 g   Saturated Fat 2 g
Cholesterol 93 mg   Percentage calories from fat 19%

Ginger Noodles with Carrots and Zucchini

Makes 4 servings

To prepare the carrots and zucchini in a flash, shred them using the julienne or shredding disk in a food processor. Otherwise, shred them on the largest holes of a hand grater.

12 ounces Japanese udon noodles or no-yolk noodles

3 tablespoons vegetable or chicken broth

3 tablespoons seasoned rice wine vinegar

1½ tablespoons teriyaki sauce

2 teaspoons Asian sesame oil

2 tablespoons minced fresh cilantro

1 tablespoon grated fresh ginger

1 teaspoon brown sugar

2 to 3 drops hot red pepper sauce

3 medium carrots, shredded

1 small zucchini, shredded

2 teaspoons toasted sesame seeds

1. In a large pot of boiling salted water, cook noodles 8 to 10 minutes, until tender but still firm.

2. Meanwhile, in a large bowl, whisk together broth, vinegar, teriyaki sauce, sesame oil, cilantro, ginger, brown sugar, and hot sauce.

3. Drain noodles and place in bowl; toss to coat. Add carrots and zucchini; toss to mix well. Sprinkle sesame seeds on top. Serve warm at room temperature.

PER SERVING   Calories 364   Total Fat 5 g   Saturated Fat 1 g
Cholesterol 13 mg   Percentage calories from fat 12%

Little Ears with White Beans

Makes 4 servings

12 ounces orechiette or small elbow macaroni

2 teaspoons olive oil

1 cup chopped fresh fennel or celery

1 cup diced red potato

2 garlic cloves, minced

½ teaspoon crushed hot red pepper

½ teaspoon dried thyme

¼ teaspoon salt

¼ teaspoon freshly ground black pepper

1 (14½-ounce) can diced tomatoes, drained

½ cup chicken broth

1 tablespoon fresh lemon juice

1 (15-ounce) can white beans, rinsed and drained

2 tablespoons chopped kalamata olives

1. In a large pot of boiling salted water, cook orechiette 10 to 12 minutes, until tender.

2. Meanwhile, in a large nonstick skillet, heat oil over medium-high heat. Add fennel, potato, garlic, hot pepper, thyme, salt, and black pepper. Cook, stirring often, 4 to 5 minutes, until vegetables are tender.

3. Add tomatoes, broth, and lemon juice. Bring to a boil; reduce heat to low. Stir in beans and olives. Cook until heated through, 4 to 5 minutes.

4. To serve, drain pasta and place in a large bowl. Spoon sauce on top and toss gently to combine.

PER SERVING   Calories 468   Total Fat 6 g   Saturated Fat 1 g
Cholesterol 0 mg   Percentage calories from fat 11%

Pappardelle with Chicken and Parsley

Makes 4 servings

12 ounces pappardelle or wide no-yolk noodles

2 teaspoons olive oil

2 garlic cloves, minced

½ pound skinless boneless chicken breasts, cut into thin strips

½ teaspoon dried thyme

½ teaspoon salt

¼ teaspoon paprika

1 medium red bell pepper, cut into thin strips

1 medium green bell pepper, cut into thin strips

½ cup chopped flat-leaf parsley

1 tablespoon capers, rinsed and finely chopped

¼ teaspoon crushed hot red pepper

1½ tablespoons balsamic vinegar

1. In a large pot of boiling salted water, cook pappardelle 10 to 12 minutes, until tender but still firm; drain.

2. Meanwhile, in a large nonstick skillet, cook garlic in 1 teaspoon oil over medium-high heat until softened, about 1 minute. Add chicken, thyme, salt, and paprika. Cook, stirring often, 4 to 5 minutes, until chicken is white in center. With a slotted spoon, remove chicken to a plate.

3. Heat remaining 1 teaspoon oil in skillet. Add bell peppers, parsley, capers, and hot pepper. Cook over medium-high heat, stirring often, 4 to 5 minutes, until peppers are tender. Stir in vinegar. Return chicken to skillet. Cook 1 to 2 minutes, tossing, until heated through. Add pasta, toss to mix, and serve.

PER SERVING   Calories 415   Total Fat 4 g   Saturated Fat 1 g
Cholesterol 33 mg   Percentage calories from fat 10%

Shells with Chunky Meat Sauce

Makes 4 servings

The rich taste in this sauce comes from the combination of ground turkey and crumbled turkey sausage. Along with a variety of fresh vegetables, this lightened classic is sure to be a crowd pleaser.

> 12 ounces large pasta shells
> 1 teaspoon olive oil
> 6 ounces ground turkey
> 6 ounces hot Italian turkey sausage, casings removed
> 1 medium onion, chopped
> 3 celery ribs, chopped
> 3 medium carrots, chopped
> 1 medium green bell pepper, chopped
> 1 (28-ounce) can crushed tomatoes
> ¼ cup tomato paste
> 2 teaspoons red wine vinegar
> 1 teaspoon dried oregano
> ½ teaspoon fennel seeds
> ½ teaspoon salt
> ¼ teaspoon freshly ground black pepper

1. In a large pot of boiling salted water, cook shells 10 to 12 minutes, until tender but still firm. Drain into a colander.

2. Meanwhile, in a large nonstick skillet, heat oil over medium heat. Add ground turkey and sausage. Cook, stirring to break up meat, 4 to 5 minutes, until no longer pink.

3. Add onion, celery, carrots, and bell pepper. Cook 3 to 5 minutes, until just tender. Stir in crushed tomatoes, tomato paste, vinegar, oregano, fennel seeds, salt, and black pepper. Bring to a boil. Reduce heat to low. Partially cover and simmer 8 to 10 minutes, until sauce thickens slightly.

4. To serve, drain shells and place in a large bowl. Pour sauce over pasta, toss lightly to mix, and serve.

PER SERVING   Calories 552   Total Fat 11 g   Saturated Fat 3 g
Cholesterol 54 mg   Percentage calories from fat 18%

Spaghettini with Red Clam Sauce

Makes 4 servings

*T*his simple sauce can work just as well with many types of seafood. Try substituting mussels or shrimp for a change of pace. When fresh tomatoes are in abundance, substitute 2 cups chopped for the canned.

12 ounces spaghettini (thin spaghetti)

2 dozen littleneck clams, scrubbed clean

1 tablespoon olive oil

2 garlic cloves, minced

1 cup chopped fresh fennel

½ cup chopped shallots

1 (28-ounce) can diced tomatoes, drained

½ cup finely chopped fresh basil or 1½ teaspoons dried

2 tablespoons grated Parmesan cheese

1. In a large pot of boiling water, cook spaghettini 8 to 10 minutes, until tender but still firm.

2. Meanwhile, in a large skillet, bring 1 inch of water to a boil over high heat. Add clams, cover, and steam until they open, 3 to 5 minutes. Discard any clams that do not open.

3. Heat oil in a large nonstick skillet over medium-high heat. Add garlic, fennel, and shallots. Cook, stirring often, 3 to 5 minutes, until tender. Stir in tomatoes and basil. Simmer 5 minutes, until sauce thickens slightly. Stir in clams. Toss gently to combine.

4. To serve, drain pasta and place in a large bowl. Top with clam sauce. Sprinkle with cheese and serve at once.

PER SERVING   Calories 487   Total Fat 7 g   Saturated Fat 1 g
Cholesterol 33 mg   Percentage calories from fat 13%

Tortellini with Tomato-Basil Rouille

Makes 4 servings

Make sure that for this dish you buy plain dried tomatoes, not the ones packed in oil, which are loaded with fat. This rouille is also great served as an appetizer on crostini.

12 dry-pack sun-dried tomato halves
½ cup boiling water
1 (9-ounce) package fresh cheese tortellini
2 cups loosely packed fresh basil leaves
2 tablespoons grated provolone cheese
1 tablespoon capers, rinsed and finely chopped
1 teaspoon olive oil
1 teaspoon red wine vinegar
¼ teaspoon salt
¼ teaspoon fresh ground black pepper

1. Place tomatoes in a small heatproof bowl. Cover with boiling water and set aside 3 to 5 minutes to soften slightly. Drain tomatoes, reserving ⅓ cup water.

2. In a large pot of boiling salted water, cook tortellini 4 to 6 minutes, until tender but still firm.

3. Meanwhile, place tomatoes with reserved soaking water and basil in a food processor. Process until finely chopped. Transfer to a large serving bowl. Add provolone cheese, capers, olive oil, vinegar, salt, and pepper. Toss to mix rouille well.

4. Drain tortellini and add to bowl. Toss to mix well and serve at once.

PER SERVING   Calories 271   Total Fat 7 g   Saturated Fat 3 g
Cholesterol 29 mg   Percentage calories from fat 23%

Ziti with Ricotta and Sautéed Vegetables

Makes 4 servings

Nonfat ricotta cheese and lemon juice make this dish a light, creamy treat. Choose whatever vegetables are in season to add variety.

12 ounces ziti
2 teaspoons olive oil
2 small zucchini, cut into thin strips
½ pound green beans, cut into 2-inch pieces
2 medium carrots, cut into thin strips
2 scallions, cut into 1-inch pieces
2 garlic cloves, minced
1 (15-ounce) container nonfat ricotta cheese
2 tablespoons fresh lemon juice
2 tablespoons chicken broth or water
2 tablespoons chopped fresh basil or parsley
¼ teaspoon freshly ground black pepper
Pinch nutmeg

1. In a large pot of boiling salted water, cook ziti 10 to 12 minutes, until tender but still firm.

2. Meanwhile, in a large nonstick skillet, heat oil over medium-high heat. Add zucchini, green beans, carrots, scallions, and garlic. Cook, stirring often, 5 to 7 minutes, until vegetables are tender.

3. In a large serving bowl, combine ricotta, lemon juice, broth, basil, pepper, and nutmeg. Mix well. Drain ziti and add to bowl. Add sautéed vegetables, toss to mix well, and serve at once.

PER SERVING   Calories 480   Total Fat 4 g   Saturated Fat 1 g
Cholesterol 0 mg   Percentage calories from fat 7%

Poultry Pronto

When it comes to light and low-fat, chicken and turkey lead the pack. With skin removed, these meats have become the first choice of health-conscious diners both at home and in restaurants. As a food writer, it is fun to slip these birds into some dishes originally intended for red meats, and to develop new ways to use these birds, so variety doesn't lag at the dinner table.

One wonderful fallout from the popularity of chicken and turkey is the many ways they are now found packaged in supermarkets. There are cutlets and breasts, legs and thighs, on and off the bone, not to speak of the variety of ground poultry and sausages. Sometimes it's hard to find a whole bird. Of course, for speed, these convenient cuts are the most appropriate—and the lowest in fat. I've included recipes for most of these cuts, as well as for a few that call for leftover chicken, perfect for when you purchase a supermarket rotisserie or barbecued chicken, and have a little meat left over. I'll show you how to stretch it and keep your nutritional balance intact.

Whether you opt for Broiled Chicken Parmigiana, Red Hot Chicken Kabobs, Chicken Egg Rolls, Baked Walnut Turkey Tenders, or Creamy Turkey Sausage and Spinach Sauce over Linguine, here you'll find all manner of chicken and turkey prepared low in fat and ready pronto!

Broiled Chicken Parmigiana

Makes 4 servings

To cut the time and fat in this dish the chicken is broiled instead of pan-fried in bread crumbs and butter. Make sure to use thin chicken cutlets to ensure that the chicken will be completely cooked through by the time the cheese melts.

4 thin chicken cutlets (3 ounces each)

½ cup fat-free Italian dressing

1 cup mushroom-flavored spaghetti sauce

1 medium tomato, thinly sliced

½ cup shredded low-fat mozzarella cheese

1 tablespoon grated Parmesan cheese

1 teaspoon dried basil

1. Preheat broiler. Line a broiler pan with aluminum foil. Place chicken in a medium bowl. Add dressing and toss to coat. Let stand 5 minutes.

2. Remove chicken from dressing and arrange on pan. Broil chicken 4 to 6 inches from heat 3 minutes.

3. Turn chicken over and top each cutlet with equal amounts of sauce, tomato, mozzarella cheese, Parmesan cheese, and basil. Broil 4 to 6 minutes longer, until chicken is no longer pink in center and cheese is melted.

PER SERVING   Calories 217   Total Fat 6 g   Saturated Fat 2 g
Cholesterol 55 mg   Percentage calories from fat 25%

Tex-Mex Chicken Cutlets

Makes 4 servings

1 tablespoon reduced-calorie margarine

1 cup boiling water

2 cups prepared stuffing mix

½ cup canned or frozen corn kernels

¼ cup finely chopped scallions

2 tablespoons canned chopped green chiles

½ teaspoon chili powder

4 thin chicken cutlets (4 to 5 ounces each)

1 cup medium salsa

½ cup shredded nonfat Monterey Jack cheese

1. Preheat broiler. Place margarine in a medium heatproof bowl. Pour on boiling water and stir until melted. Add stuffing, corn, scallions, chiles, and chili powder. Mix well.

2. Place chicken on a flat work surface; pound gently to flatten evenly. Place equal amounts of stuffing onto bottom half of each cutlet. Roll up from bottom to enclose filling. Secure with toothpicks if necessary.

3. Place chicken in a small nonstick baking pan. Spoon ¼ cup salsa over each cutlet. Broil 4 to 6 inches from heat 6 to 8 minutes, until chicken begins to brown at edges. Sprinkle cheese over top. Broil 2 to 3 minutes longer, until cheese melts and chicken is white in center. Serve hot.

PER SERVING   Calories 339   Total Fat 4 g   Saturated Fat 1 g
Cholesterol 66 mg   Percentage calories from fat 12%

Chicken with Chickpeas and Pine Nuts

Makes 4 servings

*C*alled ceci *in Italian, chickpeas are combined with chicken and other savory ingredients for a substantial dish that's good on its own or with rice or pasta.*

1 teaspoon olive oil

4 skinless boneless chicken breast halves (about 4 ounces each)

½ teaspoon garlic powder

½ teaspoon dried thyme

¼ teaspoon salt

1 tablespoon pine nuts

1 (16-ounce) can chickpeas, drained

1 (7-ounce) jar roasted red peppers, cut into thin strips

½ cup chicken broth

⅓ cup thinly sliced arugula

1 tablespoon balsamic vinegar

¼ teaspoon crushed hot red pepper

1. Heat oil in a large nonstick skillet over medium-high heat. Add chicken; season with garlic powder, thyme, and salt. Cook 4 to 5 minutes on each side, until browned. Remove to a plate.

2. Add pine nuts to skillet and cook, stirring constantly, 1 minute to toast lightly. Stir in chickpeas, roasted peppers, broth, arugula, vinegar, and hot pepper. Bring to a boil; reduce heat to low.

3. Return chicken to skillet. Cook 5 to 7 minutes longer, stirring to coat with sauce, until chicken is white throughout but still juicy.

PER SERVING   Calories 246   Total Fat 5 g   Saturated Fat 1 g
Cholesterol 66 mg   Percentage calories from fat 21%

Chicken Couscous

Makes 4 servings

1 teaspoon olive oil

2 bell peppers, red and yellow, cut into thin strips

1 cup chopped scallions

2 garlic cloves, minced

¾ pound skinless boneless chicken breast halves

½ cup chicken broth

1 medium tomato, chopped

¼ cup chopped dried apricots

¼ cup chopped pitted prunes

2 teaspoons chili powder

¾ teaspoon ground coriander

¼ teaspoon ground cloves

¼ teaspoon ground ginger

2 teaspoons fresh lemon juice

1 ⅓ cups prepared quick-cooking couscous

1. In a large nonstick skillet, heat oil. Add bell peppers, scallions, and garlic. Cook, stirring often, 2 to 3 minutes, until peppers are crisp-tender.

2. Add chicken to skillet. Cook, turning, 3 to 4 minutes on each side, until browned. Stir in broth, tomato, dried apricots, and prunes. Cook 2 minutes. Stir in chili powder, coriander, cloves, and ginger. Cook 5 minutes longer, until chicken is white in center. Stir in lemon juice.

3. To serve, fluff couscous and place on a large platter. Top with chicken mixture and any remaining sauce. Pass harissa or another hot sauce on the side.

PER SERVING   Calories 412   Total Fat 3 g   Saturated Fat 1 g
Cholesterol 49 mg   Percentage calories from fat 7%

Creamy Chicken Curry

Makes 4 servings

½ cup nonfat plain yogurt

⅓ cup nonfat mayonnaise

2 tablespoons minced chives

1 teaspoon lime juice

½ teaspoon curry powder

½ teaspoon ground ginger

Pinch ground red pepper

1 teaspoon Asian sesame oil

¾ pound skinless boneless chicken breasts, cut into long, thin strips

½ teaspoon chili powder

½ teaspoon garlic powder

¼ teaspoon salt

1 small red bell pepper, chopped

2 tablespoons chopped cilantro or parsley

1. In a small bowl, combine yogurt, mayonnaise, chives, lime juice, curry powder, ginger, and red pepper. Mix to blend well. Set curry sauce aside.

2. In a large nonstick skillet, heat oil over medium-high heat. Add chicken strips. Sprinkle on chili powder, garlic powder, and salt and toss to coat. Add bell pepper and cook, stirring often, 4 to 6 minutes, until chicken is no longer pink.

3. Reduce heat to low. Gradually stir in curry sauce. Cook, stirring constantly, 2 minutes, until heated through, but do not let boil or sauce may curdle. Serve hot, garnished with cilantro.

PER SERVING   Calories 144   Total Fat 2 g   Saturated Fat 1 g
Cholesterol 50 mg   Percentage calories from fat 16%

Red Hot Chicken Kabobs

Makes 4 servings

¼ cup packed dark brown sugar

1 tablespoon red wine vinegar

2 teaspoons chili powder

2 teaspoons peanut oil

1 teaspoon paprika

½ teaspoon ground ginger

½ teaspoon salt

¼ to ½ teaspoon hot red pepper sauce, or more to taste

¾ pound skinless boneless chicken breasts, cut into 1-inch pieces

5 scallions, cut into 1-inch pieces

1 medium red bell pepper, cut into 1-inch pieces

1 medium green bell pepper, cut into 1-inch pieces

1. Preheat broiler or light a hot fire in a barbecue grill.

2. In a large bowl, combine brown sugar, vinegar, chili powder, peanut oil, paprika, ginger, salt, and hot sauce. Add chicken and toss to mix well. Let marinate at room temperature 5 to 10 minutes.

3. Thread equal amounts of chicken, scallions, and bell peppers into 8 metal or water-soaked bamboo skewers; reserve marinade.

4. Broil or grill kabobs, turning and brushing with reserved marinade, 6 minutes. Continue to cook, turning, until chicken is browned outside and white in center, 2 to 4 minutes longer.

PER SERVING   Calories 192   Total Fat 4 g   Saturated Fat 1 g
Cholesterol 49 mg   Percentage calories from fat 17%

Orange Broiled Chicken

Makes 4 servings

*A*dding *a quick broiling sauce to your recipe collection can come in quite handy for last-minute grilling or broiling. This sauce works just as nicely on fish and vegetables. The all-fruit spreads are great to use instead of sugar-packed marmalades.*

½ cup orange all-fruit spread

2 tablespoons grated onion

2 tablespoons orange juice

1 tablespoon Dijon mustard

½ teaspoon dried tarragon

¼ teaspoon ground ginger

¼ teaspoon salt

4 skinless boneless chicken breast halves (3 ounces each)

1. Preheat broiler. Use a nonstick broiler rack or coat broiling pan with nonstick cooking spray.

2. In a small bowl, combine all-fruit spread, onion, orange juice, mustard, tarragon, ginger, and salt. Mix well.

3. Place chicken on prepared pan and brush with half of sauce. Broil about 6 inches from heat 5 minutes, until lightly browned. Turn chicken over and brush with remaining sauce. Broil 5 to 7 minutes longer, until chicken is browned outside and white throughout but still juicy in center.

PER SERVING   Calories 188   Total Fat 1 g   Saturated Fat <1 g
Cholesterol 49 mg   Percentage calories from fat 5%

Braised Chicken Drumsticks with Peas and Mushrooms

Makes 4 servings

1 ½ pounds skinless chicken drumsticks
½ teaspoon salt
¼ teaspoon freshly ground black pepper
1 teaspoon olive oil
1 pound mushrooms, quartered
1 medium onion, chopped
½ teaspoon dried thyme
½ teaspoon dried rosemary, crushed
⅓ cup chicken broth
⅓ cup apple juice
1 (14½-ounce) can diced tomatoes, drained
1 (10-ounce) box frozen peas, thawed

1. Season chicken drumsticks with salt and pepper. In a large non-stick skillet, heat oil over medium-high heat. Add chicken; cook, turning, until lightly browned all over, 4 to 6 minutes. Remove to a plate.

2. Add mushrooms, onion, thyme, and rosemary to skillet. Cook, stirring often, 3 to 5 minutes, until mushrooms are lightly browned.

3. Stir in broth, apple juice, tomatoes, and peas. Bring to a boil. Return chicken to skillet. Reduce heat to low, cover, and simmer 8 to 10 minutes, stirring often, until chicken is tender, with no trace of pink near bone. Season sauce with additional salt and pepper to taste before serving.

PER SERVING   Calories 269   Total Fat 6 g   Saturated Fat 1 g
Cholesterol 83 mg   Percentage calories from fat 20%

Coconut Chicken with Creamy Spinach Sauce

Makes 4 servings

14 fat-free saltine crackers

3 tablespoons shredded unsweetened coconut

1 teaspoon grated lemon zest

Pinch ground white pepper

2 egg whites

4 skinless boneless chicken thighs (3 ounces each)

1 teaspoon olive oil

1 cup minced scallions

2 garlic cloves, minced

1 cup evaporated skimmed milk

1 cup thawed frozen chopped spinach, squeezed dry

1 teaspoon lemon juice

Pinch nutmeg

10 ounces wide no-yolk noodles

1. In a food processor, combine crackers, coconut, lemon zest, and white pepper. Process until ground to fine crumbs. Place crumbs on a large piece of wax paper.

2. In a shallow bowl, lightly beat egg whites. Dip chicken first in egg whites, then dredge in cracker crumbs to coat both sides.

3. In a large nonstick skillet, heat oil over medium heat. Add chicken; cook 5 minutes on each side, until browned outside and no longer pink in center. Remove and cover to keep warm.

4. Add scallions and garlic to skillet. Cook 2 minutes, or until scallions wilt and garlic is softened and fragrant. Stir in milk, spinach, lemon juice, and nutmeg. Simmer 3 to 5 minutes longer, stirring constantly, until sauce thickens slightly.

5. In a large pot of boiling salted water, cook noodles 10 to 12 minutes, until tender but still firm. Drain well and transfer to a serving platter. Arrange chicken over noodles and top with sauce. Serve at once.

PER SERVING   Calories *497*   Total Fat *8 g*   Saturated Fat *3 g*
Cholesterol *73 mg*   Percentage calories from fat *15%*

Grecian Chicken Thighs

Makes 4 servings

A strong-flavored cheese like feta goes a long way even in small amounts. To vary the taste here, try using different varieties of feta, such as pepper-flecked or with dry-pack sun-dried tomatoes and basil.

4 skinless boneless chicken thighs (about 3 ounces each)
½ teaspoon dried basil
¼ teaspoon salt
¼ teaspoon freshly ground black pepper
1 teaspoon olive oil
1 medium red bell pepper, chopped
2 garlic cloves, minced
¼ cup crumbled feta cheese
2 tablespoons thinly sliced pitted ripe olives
1 tablespoon balsamic vinegar

1. Season chicken thighs on both sides with basil, salt, and black pepper. Heat oil in a large nonstick skillet. Add chicken and cook over medium-high heat 3 to 5 minutes on each side, until nicely browned. Transfer to a plate.

2. Add bell pepper and garlic to skillet; cook, stirring often, 2 to 3 minutes, until tender. Stir in feta cheese, olives, and vinegar.

3. Return chicken to skillet. Cook 2 to 3 minutes, spooning sauce over chicken, until juices run clear when thigh is pricked. Serve hot.

PER SERVING   Calories 311   Total Fat 7g   Saturated Fat 2 g
Cholesterol 78 mg   Percentage calories from fat 21%

Savory Tarragon Roast Chicken Thighs with Citrus and Soy Sauce

Makes 4 servings

Fresh citrus is a great way to increase flavor without adding a lot of fat and sodium to any recipe. I particularly like the sprightliness of lemon mixed with the sweet grassiness of tarragon. Here soy sauce contributes as much color as taste.

1½ tablespoons fresh lemon juice

1½ tablespoons orange juice

1 teaspoon grated lemon zest

2 garlic cloves, crushed through a press

2 teaspoons soy sauce

1 teaspoon dried tarragon

½ teaspoon salt

¼ teaspoon freshly ground black pepper

1½ pounds skinless chicken thighs

1. Preheat oven to 425 degrees F. In a small bowl, mix together all ingredients except chicken until well blended.

2. Rub citrus-soy sauce mixture all over chicken. Place chicken in a small baking dish. Set in middle of oven.

3. Roast 15 to 20 minutes, turning once, until chicken is tender and juices run clear when thigh is pricked near bone.

PER SERVING   Calories 159   Total Fat 5 g   Saturated Fat 1 g
Cholesterol 104 mg   Percentage calories from fat 29%

Ginger-Glazed Chicken Wings

Makes 4 servings

*C*hicken wings are traditionally deep-fat fried. This version comes complete with all the flavor but without all the fat. Removing the skin gets rid of a lot of it. If you have a friendly butcher, ask him to prepare the wings for you to save time. Ginger and honey impart wonderful sweet-hot flair to the glaze.

2 tablespoons soy sauce

2 tablespoons fresh lemon juice

1 tablespoon chopped fresh ginger

2 to 3 drops hot red pepper sauce

1¼ pounds chicken wings, skinned and separated at joints, tips removed

¼ cup thawed frozen apple juice concentrate

2 tablespoons honey

1 teaspoon peanut oil

1. In a large bowl, combine soy sauce, 1 tablespoon lemon juice, ginger, and hot sauce. Add chicken wings; toss to coat well. Set aside for 5 to 10 minutes.

2. In a small bowl, combine apple juice concentrate, honey, and remaining 1 tablespoon lemon juice.

3. In a nonstick wok or large skillet, heat oil over medium-high heat. Add chicken wings and cook, tossing, 2 to 3 minutes, until browned.

4. Pour in apple juice mixture; cover and cook 5 minutes, still over medium-high heat. Uncover and cook, tossing, 5 minutes longer, or until chicken is cooked through and liquid is reduced to a glaze. Serve hot, at room temperature, or cold.

PER SERVING   Calories 201   Total Fat 5 g   Saturated Fat 1 g
Cholesterol 55 mg   Percentage calories from fat 21%

Grilled Chicken Burgers
with Chili-Mustard Sauce

Makes 4 servings

¼ cup nonfat mayonnaise

1 tablespoon chili sauce

1 teaspoon Dijon mustard

1 teaspoon lime juice

¾ pound lean ground chicken

¼ cup plain dry bread crumbs

¼ cup minced scallions

2 tablespoons minced cilantro

½ teaspoon dried thyme

¼ teaspoon freshly ground black pepper

Coarse (kosher) salt

4 hamburger buns

1 large tomato, cut into 8 slices

1. In a small bowl, combine mayonnaise, chili sauce, mustard, and lime juice. Blend sauce well.

2. In a medium bowl, combine ground chicken, bread crumbs, scallions, cilantro, thyme, and pepper. Mix until well blended. Shape into 4 equal patties about ½ inch thick.

3. Heat a large cast-iron or nonstick skillet over medium-high heat. Sprinkle salt lightly over bottom of pan. Add burgers and cook 5 to 6 minutes on each side, until browned outside and no longer pink in center. Reduce heat slightly if burgers start to burn. Serve in buns, topped with tomato slices and sauce.

PER SERVING   Calories 313   Total Fat 11 g   Saturated Fat 3 g
Cholesterol 71 mg   Percentage calories from fat 30%

Chicken Egg Rolls

Makes 4 servings

Instead of the deep-fat fried variety commonly found at Chinese restaurants, these tasty packets are wrapped in wonton skins and baked. Serve with Chinese mustard and bottled plum or duck sauce for dipping.

2 tablespoons chicken broth

1 teaspoon soy sauce

1 teaspoon Asian sesame oil

½ teaspoon sugar

¼ teaspoon ground ginger

1½ tablespoons cornstarch

1 cup shredded carrots

1 cup shredded zucchini

1 cup drained canned bean sprouts

½ cup finely chopped green bell pepper

2 tablespoons minced onion

½ pound shredded cooked chicken (about 1⅓ cups)

16 wonton wrappers, thawed if frozen

1. Preheat oven to 375 degrees F. In a small bowl, combine broth, soy sauce, oil, sugar, and ginger. Whisk in cornstarch until dissolved. Set sauce aside.

2. Coat a large nonstick skillet with nonstick cooking spray; heat skillet. Add carrots, zucchini, bean sprouts, bell pepper, and onion. Cook, stirring often, 2 minutes. Add shredded chicken and reserved sauce. Cook 2 minutes longer, until heated through and thickened slightly.

3. Place wonton wrappers on a flat work surface. Place 3 to 4 tablespoons chicken mixture on bottom half of each wrapper. Fold both sides toward center; roll up tightly from bottom. Place rolls seam side down on a nonstick baking sheet.

4. Bake 6 to 8 minutes, until lightly browned. Serve hot.

PER SERVING   Calories 225   Total Fat 3 g   Saturated Fat 1 g
Cholesterol 44 mg   Percentage calories from fat 13%

Chicken Tetrazzini with
Mushrooms and Broccoli

Makes 4 servings

A rich cream sauce is traditional in tetrazzini recipes. Here the dish is lightened and made for today's more healthful standards with skim milk. Fresh vegetables and herbs add additional color and interest. This recipe calls for elbow macaroni, but any leftover pasta will do; if you have 2 cups left over, by all means use it.

1 cup elbow macaroni

1 teaspoon olive oil

½ pound mushrooms, thinly sliced (2 cups)

2 cups broccoli florets

5 scallions, chopped

2 garlic cloves, minced

1⅓ cups skim milk

2 teaspoons cornstarch

1 teaspoon dried thyme

½ teaspoon dried oregano

¼ teaspoon salt

1½ cups shredded cooked chicken (about 10 ounces)

1 large plum tomato, seeded and chopped

3 tablespoons grated Parmesan cheese

1 tablespoon sliced almonds

1. Preheat oven to 375 degrees F. In a large saucepan of boiling salted water, cook macaroni until tender but still firm, 5 to 7 minutes. Drain, rinse briefly under cold running water, and drain well.

2. In a large saucepan, heat oil over medium-high heat. Add mushrooms, broccoli, scallions, and garlic. Cook, stirring often, 4 to 5 minutes, until broccoli is just tender.

3. In a small bowl, whisk together milk, cornstarch, thyme, oregano, and salt until cornstarch is dissolved. Stir milk mixture into saucepan. Cook, stirring often, 2 to 3 minutes, until sauce comes to a boil and thickens slightly. Add chicken, macaroni, and tomato; cook 1 minute. Remove from heat and spoon into a nonstick 8-inch-square baking pan.

4. Sprinkle cheese and almonds over top. Bake 8 to 10 minutes, until golden brown and bubbly.

PER SERVING   Calories 325   Total Fat 6 g   Saturated Fat 2 g
Cholesterol 57 mg   Percentage calories from fat 17%

Crusty Parmesan Turkey Cutlets

Makes 4 servings

½ cup seasoned dry bread crumbs

¼ cup flour

2 tablespoons grated Parmesan cheese

1 tablespoon paprika

½ teaspoon garlic powder

¼ teaspoon salt

Pinch freshly ground black pepper

¼ cup chicken broth

1 tablespoon reduced-calorie margarine

¾ pound turkey cutlets, cut into 4 equal pieces

1. Preheat oven to 400 degrees F. On a large sheet of wax paper, combine bread crumbs, flour, cheese, paprika, garlic powder, and pepper.

2. Place broth and margarine in an 8-inch-square baking pan. Place pan in oven; heat 1 to 2 minutes, until margarine melts. Remove pan from oven.

3. Dip cutlets on both sides in broth mixture. Dredge in crumbs to coat on both sides, pressing to help them stick.

4. Arrange cutlets in baking pan. Bake 7 minutes. Turn cutlets over; bake 8 to 10 minutes longer, until turkey is white throughout and crumbs are golden.

PER SERVING   Calories 209   Total Fat 3 g   Saturated Fat 1 g
Cholesterol 55 mg   Percentage calories from fat 15%

Turkey Eggplant Kabobs

Makes 4 servings

2 tablespoons honey

2 tablespoons Dijon mustard

2 teaspoons white wine vinegar

1 teaspoon rosemary, crushed

1 teaspoon Asian sesame oil

¼ teaspoon salt

¼ teaspoon freshly ground black pepper

¾ pound skinless boneless turkey breast, cut into 1-inch pieces

1 small eggplant, cut into 1-inch cubes

16 cherry tomatoes

1 medium green bell pepper, cut into 1-inch pieces

3 tablespoons fresh lemon juice

1 teaspoon salt-free lemon-herb seasoning blend

1. Preheat broiler. In a large bowl, combine honey, mustard, vinegar, rosemary, sesame oil, salt, and black pepper. Add turkey and toss to coat well. Let marinate at room temperature 5 to 10 minutes.

2. In a medium bowl, combine eggplant, tomatoes, and bell pepper. Sprinkle lemon juice and seasoning blend over vegetables; toss to mix well.

3. Thread equal amounts of turkey and vegetables on 8 metal or water-soaked bamboo skewers. Place on a rack in a broiler pan or on a grill rack sprayed with nonstick cooking spray. Broil or grill kabobs 7 to 10 minutes, turning often, until turkey is white throughout and vegetables are tender.

PER SERVING   Calories 195   Total Fat 2 g   Saturated Fat <1 g
Cholesterol 53 mg   Percentage calories from fat 9%

Turkey Apple Stir-Fry
with Brown Rice

Makes 4 servings

*A*ny *thinly sliced meat or poultry will work well in this dish. The key to perfect stir-fry success is to have all your ingredients prepared and ready to use.*

1 cup instant brown rice

2 tablespoons chicken broth or water

2 tablespoons apple juice

1 tablespoon soy sauce

1 teaspoon grated fresh ginger

1 teaspoon cider vinegar

2 tablespoons flour

½ teaspoon ground coriander

Pinch white pepper

¾ pound turkey tenderloins, cut into thin strips

1 teaspoon peanut oil

1 cup chopped scallions

1 green bell pepper, thinly sliced

1 medium apple, peeled, cored, and thinly sliced

¼ cup golden raisins

1. In a small saucepan, bring 1 cup water to a boil. Stir in rice. Cover, remove from heat, and let stand at least 5 minutes.

2. Meanwhile, in a small bowl, combine broth, apple juice, soy sauce, ginger, and vinegar. Set sauce aside.

3. In a 1-gallon plastic food storage bag, combine flour, coriander, and white pepper. Add turkey strips, seal bag, and toss to coat with flour.

4. Remove turkey from bag; shake off excess flour. In a nonstick wok or large skillet, heat oil over medium-high heat. Add turkey to wok and stir-fry until golden brown and no longer pink, 3 to 4 minutes. Remove turkey to a plate.

5. Add scallions, bell pepper, apple slices, and raisins to wok. Stir-fry 2 to 4 minutes, until bell pepper is crisp-tender. Return turkey to wok. Add sauce and cook, stirring, 2 minutes longer. Serve hot over steamed brown rice.

PER SERVING   Calories 266   Total Fat 3 g   Saturated Fat <1 g
Cholesterol 53 mg   Percentage calories from fat 9%

Turkey with Mushrooms and Almonds

Makes 4 servings

3 tablespoons sliced almonds

¾ pound turkey breast cutlets, cut into 4 equal pieces

½ teaspoon dried thyme

¼ teaspoon salt

¼ teaspoon freshly ground black pepper

1 small onion, finely chopped

½ pound mushrooms, thinly sliced

½ cup chicken broth

2 tablespoons dry white wine or nonalcoholic white wine

2 tablespoons chopped fresh parsley

1. Coat a large nonstick skillet with nonstick cooking spray; heat skillet. Add almonds; cook, stirring constantly 1 to 2 minutes, until golden. Remove from skillet and set aside.

2. Season turkey on both sides with thyme, salt, and pepper. Spray skillet with nonstick spray again; heat skillet. Add turkey and cook over medium-high heat 3 minutes on each side, until golden brown and tender. Transfer turkey to a serving platter; cover with foil to keep warm.

3. Add onion to skillet and cook 2 minutes. Add mushrooms; cook, stirring often, 2 to 3 minutes, until mushrooms are tender. Pour in broth and wine. Bring to a boil and cook 2 minutes longer, or until liquid is reduced by half.

4. Spoon mushroom sauce over turkey. Serve, garnished with toasted almonds and chopped parsley.

PER SERVING   Calories 149   Total Fat 4 g   Saturated Fat <1 g
Cholesterol 53 mg   Percentage calories from fat 22%

Baked Walnut Turkey Tenders

Makes 4 servings

Turkey tenders provide an easy way to make finger-size food your family will love to pick up on the run on busy nights. A small amount of chopped walnuts and cornmeal make the coating tasty and crunchy.

2 large egg whites
¼ cup yellow cornmeal
2 tablespoons finely chopped walnuts
2 tablespoons chopped fresh parsley
¼ teaspoon garlic powder
¼ teaspoon salt
⅛ teaspoon dried thyme
Pinch cayenne
¾ pound turkey tenders

1. Preheat oven to 400 degrees F. Place egg whites in a shallow bowl and beat lightly with a fork.

2. On a large piece of wax paper, combine cornmeal, walnuts, parsley, garlic powder, salt, thyme, and cayenne. Mix well.

3. Dip turkey tenders in egg whites. Place on wax paper and toss to coat on both sides with cornmeal mixture, pressing firmly to help coating stick to turkey.

4. Place tenders on a large nonstick baking sheet. Bake 5 minutes. Turn tenders over and bake 5 to 7 minutes longer, until turkey is golden brown outside and white throughout.

PER SERVING   Calories 164   Total Fat 3 g   Saturated Fat <1 g
Cholesterol 53 mg   Percentage calories from fat 19%

Creamy Turkey Sausage and Spinach Sauce over Linguine

Makes 8 servings

This multipurpose sauce can be used in many ways. Try serving over rice, baked potatoes, or even spooned into bell pepper shells and baked with shredded cheese on top.

½ cup dry-pack sun-dried tomato halves

1 pound hot Italian turkey sausage, casings removed

1 teaspoon olive oil

½ pound fresh mushrooms, sliced

½ cup chopped celery

½ cup chopped onion

2 garlic cloves, minced

2½ cups thinly sliced escarole or fresh spinach

1 (10¾-ounce) can condensed reduced-fat cream of mushroom soup

½ cup tomato sauce

¼ teaspoon freshly ground black pepper

1 pound dried linguine

1. Place dried tomatoes in a small heatproof bowl. Cover with boiling water; let stand 10 minutes, until plump. Drain and set aside.

2. Meanwhile, coat a large nonstick skillet with nonstick cooking spray; heat skillet. Add sausage and cook over medium-high heat, stirring often to break meat into small pieces, 6 to 8 minutes, until no longer pink. With a slotted spoon, remove to a plate.

3. Add oil to skillet and heat. Add mushrooms, celery, onions, and garlic. Cook over medium-high heat, stirring often, 2 to 3 minutes, until just tender. Add sausage, escarole, cream of mushroom soup, tomato sauce, dried tomatoes, pepper, and ½ cup water. Simmer, stirring often, 5 to 6 minutes longer, until sauce is heated through.

4. Meanwhile, in a large saucepan of boiling salted water, cook linguine until tender but still firm, 10 to 12 minutes. Drain and transfer to a large serving bowl. Pour sauce over pasta, toss to mix, and serve.

PER SERVING   Calories 364   Total Fat 9 g   Saturated Fat 2 g
Cholesterol 34 mg   Percentage calories from fat 22%

Ground Turkey Stir-Fry with Mixed Vegetables

Makes 4 servings

1 cup reduced-sodium chicken broth

2 tablespoons teriyaki sauce

1 tablespoon honey

1 tablespoon cornstarch

2 to 3 drops hot red pepper sauce

¾ pound lean ground turkey

1 teaspoon peanut oil

1 cup scallion pieces (1-inch)

2 tablespoons finely chopped fresh ginger

2 cups broccoli florets

2 cups snow peas

1 large red bell pepper, cut into thin strips

1 cup canned baby corn, rinsed and drained

1. In a small bowl, combine broth, teriyaki sauce, honey, cornstarch, and pepper sauce. Mix well; set sauce aside.

2. Coat a large nonstick skillet with nonstick cooking spray; heat skillet. Add ground turkey; cook, stirring often to break meat into smaller pieces, 4 to 5 minutes, until no longer pink. With a slotted spoon, transfer to a plate.

3. Add oil to skillet and heat. Add scallions and ginger; cook 2 minutes. Add broccoli, snow peas, and bell peppers; cook, stirring often, 4 to 5 minutes, until vegetables are crisp-tender.

4. Stir in sauce and cook 1 minute, until thickened. Add turkey and baby corn. Cook 2 minutes, until heated through. Serve hot.

PER SERVING   Calories 256   Total Fat 9 g   Saturated Fat 2 g
Cholesterol 62 mg   Percentage calories from fat 30%

Fast and Lean Meats

For most people who move to a low-fat diet, the hardest thing to give up is meat. Well, with the recipes in this chapter, you don't have to. Here you can enjoy moderation rather than deprivation. Smaller amounts of well-trimmed beef, veal, pork, and even lamb combined with larger servings of complex carbohydrates allow a hearty meal with a nutritional value that is still at or below 30 percent calories from fat.

There are sound reasons not to avoid meat entirely. It does contain important nutritional benefits, such as iron, zinc, and B vitamins. The only problem is the animal fat. When you are purchasing meat, make sure to look for two key words: loin and round. These contain much less internal fat than many other cuts, such as chuck sirloin. A good butcher—in a specialty meat market or in your supermarket—can be a big help in saving time by removing all visible fat from your meat before you even get it home. In case you do have to do it yourself, it's well worth equipping your kitchen with a good, sharp boning knife or chef's knife for trimming.

The right cooking techniques can effectively reduce fat without sacrificing flavor. Sautéing, stir-frying, and broiling are quick-cooking methods that seal in natural juices and produce terrific results. Sauces and quick marinades are also helpful to add flavor and tenderize without adding extra fat.

Steak Fajitas with Sweet Pepper Salsa

Makes 4 servings

1 medium green bell pepper, chopped

1 medium yellow or red bell pepper, chopped

1 medium tomato, chopped

½ cup chopped red onion

1 tablespoon canned chopped green chiles

1 teaspoon red wine vinegar

½ teaspoon Worcestershire sauce

½ teaspoon salt

¼ teaspoon ground cumin

1 teaspoon olive oil

10 ounces trimmed sirloin steak, cut into thin strips

½ teaspoon chili powder

½ cup bottled tomato salsa

¼ cup nonfat sour cream

4 (10-inch) flour tortillas, warmed

1. In a small bowl, combine green and yellow bell peppers, tomatoes, red onion, chiles, vinegar, Worcestershire, salt, and cumin. Stir to mix well. Set sweet pepper salsa aside.

2. In a large nonstick skillet, heat oil over medium-high heat. Add steak strips, sprinkle with chili powder, and cook, stirring often, 2 to 3 minutes for medium-rare. Stir in bottled salsa and toss to coat.

3. Divide steak among tortillas. Top each with 2 tablespoons pepper salsa and 1 tablespoon sour cream. Roll up to enclose filling. Pass remaining pepper salsa.

PER SERVING   Calories 328   Total Fat 9 g   Saturated Fat 2 g
Cholesterol 43 mg   Percentage calories from fat 24%

Orange-Glazed Flank Steak

Makes 4 servings

Envelopes of soup mix are mixed with all-fruit spread to make a flavorful marinade for the flank steak. Onion soup can be substituted for the vegetable soup mix if desired. Recipe can also be done on the grill instead of the broiler.

1 (1.4-ounce) envelope vegetable soup and recipe mix
½ cup orange all-fruit spread
½ cup apple juice
1 pound lean flank steak
½ teaspoon garlic powder
½ teaspoon freshly ground black pepper
1 medium red onion, thinly sliced and separated into rings
4 cups loosely packed fresh spinach leaves
1 large navel orange, peeled and sliced

1. Preheat broiler. In a small bowl, combine soup mix, fruit spread, and apple juice. Mix well until blended.

2. Score flank steak lightly on both sides. Place in a shallow roasting pan and season on both sides with garlic powder and pepper. Pour soup mixture over steak; turn meat over to coat on both sides. Scatter red onion rings over top.

3. Broil steak 4 to 6 inches from heat 5 to 6 minutes on each side for medium rare. To serve, carve steak into thin slices. Divide spinach and orange slices evenly among 4 plates. Top with steak slices. Spoon any remaining sauce in pan over steak and serve.

PER SERVING   Calories 349   Total Fat 8 g   Saturated Fat 4 g
Cholesterol 53 mg   Percentage calories from fat 21%

Vegetable-Stuffed Flank Steak

Makes 8 servings

Not only is this dish tasty, it slices to reveal a colorful filling of fresh vegetables. To accomplish this, a pocket is cut into the steak; if you have a friendly butcher, ask him to do this for you. For easier slicing after cooking, let the steak stand at least 5 minutes before carving. Serve with roast potatoes and a tossed salad.

1½ pounds trimmed lean flank steak, as thick as possible

1 cup spicy mixed vegetable juice

1 tablespoon reduced-calorie margarine

1 large onion, chopped (1¼ cups)

3 or 4 large carrots, peeled and finely diced (1¼ cups)

2 large celery ribs, finely diced (1 cup)

1 cup thawed frozen chopped spinach, squeezed dry

1 cup seasoned dry bread crumbs

3 tablespoons chicken broth

2 teaspoons Worcestershire sauce

½ teaspoon dried thyme

½ teaspoon dried basil

¼ teaspoon crushed rosemary

¼ teaspoon freshly ground black pepper

1. Preheat broiler or prepare outdoor grill. Holding meat flat on a cutting board, cut a deep pocket horizontally through center of steak, extending to within 1 inch of sides of meat. If steak thins out considerably, stop at that point so meat is not torn. Place steak in a shallow pan and pour vegetable juice over meat. Set aside.

2. In a large nonstick skillet, melt margarine over medium-high heat. Add onion, carrots, and celery. Cook, stirring often, 3 to 4 minutes, until softened. Remove from heat and stir in spinach, bread crumbs, broth, Worcestershire, thyme, basil, rosemary, and pepper.

3. Remove steak from the pan and reserve the vegetable juice. Stuff the steak evenly with the vegetable mixture. Secure with either toothpicks or skewers.

4. Broil or grill steak 4 to 5 minutes on each side for medium rare, or to desired doneness, brushing often with remaining vegetable juice.

PER SERVING   Calories 225   Total Fat 7 g   Saturated Fat 3 g
Cholesterol 43 mg   Percentage calories from fat 30%

Filet Mignon with
Dried Tomato Topping

Makes 4 servings

Filet mignon is the leanest cut of beef, but it is dear, so save this recipe for a special occasion. I like to serve it over an herbed rice pilaf with steamed asparagus and sautéed mushrooms. The tomato topping here is also great on baked potatoes. Keep in mind that because it is so lean, filet mignon is tenderest, juiciest, and most flavorful if eaten on the rare side.

½ cup dry-pack sun-dried tomatoes

1 cup boiling water

2 tablespoons crumbled feta cheese

2 tablespoons chopped fresh basil

2 garlic cloves, minced

1 teaspoon balsamic vinegar

¼ teaspoon freshly ground black pepper

4 slices white bread (about 2 ounces each)

4 filet mignon steaks, cut 1½ inches thick (4 to 5 ounces each)

1. Preheat broiler. Coat a broiler pan with nonstick cooking spray. Place dried tomatoes in a small heatproof bowl. Cover with boiling water and let stand 5 minutes, until somewhat softened. Drain; coarsely chop tomatoes.

2. In a small bowl, place tomatoes, cheese, basil, garlic, vinegar, and pepper. Toss to combine.

3. Place bread slices on pan and broil about 4 inches from heat 1 to 2 minutes on each side, until lightly toasted. Cut each bread slice diagonally into 4 triangles and set aside.

4. Place filets mignons on broiler pan. Broil about 4 inches from heat 5 minutes. Turn over and broil 2 minutes. Spoon equal amounts of tomato topping over steaks. Broil 1 to 2 minutes longer for rare, 2 to 3 minutes longer for medium rare, or to desired doneness. Serve over toast points.

PER SERVING   Calories 402   Total Fat 13 g   Saturated Fat 5 g
Cholesterol 85 mg   Percentage calories from fat 30%

Meatballs in Marinara Sauce

Makes 4 servings

Serve these savory meatballs over pasta, or with sides of roasted potatoes and steamed broccoli or braised broccoli rabe. Or form them into tiny meatballs and serve on toothpicks as a hot appetizer.

1 teaspoon reduced-calorie margarine

1/3 cup minced onion

2 garlic cloves, minced

1/4 pound lean ground beef

1/4 pound lean ground veal

1/4 pound lean ground pork

1/4 cup skim milk

1/3 cup seasoned dry bread crumbs

1 large egg white, lightly beaten

1/2 teaspoon dried thyme

1/2 teaspoon dried oregano

1/4 teaspoon nutmeg

1/4 teaspoon salt

2 cups fat-free marinara sauce

1. Preheat broiler. In a small nonstick skillet, melt margarine over medium-high heat. Add onion and garlic; cook, stirring often, 2 to 3 minutes, or until softened.

2. Scrape onion and garlic into a mixing bowl. Add beef, veal, pork, milk, bread crumbs, egg white, thyme, oregano, nutmeg, and salt. Mix to blend well. Shape into 1½-inch balls.

3. Place meatballs on a large nonstick baking sheet. Broil about 6 inches from heat, turning often, 10 to 12 minutes, or until meatballs are nicely browned outside.

4. In a large saucepan, bring marinara sauce to a simmer. Add hot meatballs and simmer 5 to 10 minutes to blend flavors.

PER SERVING   Calories 234   Total Fat 8 g   Saturated Fat 3 g
Cholesterol 56 mg   Percentage calories from fat 30%

Sautéed Veal with Olives, Peppers, and Tomatoes

Makes 4 servings

*T*hin *turkey or chicken cutlets or pork scallops can be used in place of the veal here, if you like. Crunchy red, yellow, and green bell peppers give this dish wonderful color and flavor. Serve over wide no-yolk noodles or with wild rice.*

3 tablespoons flour

¼ teaspoon salt

¼ teaspoon freshly ground black pepper

4 thin veal cutlets (3 to 4 ounces each)

3 medium bell peppers (preferably 1 green, 1 red, and 1 yellow),
       cut into thin strips

3 scallions, chopped

2 garlic cloves, minced

1 (14½-ounce) can diced tomatoes, drained

1 cup reduced-sodium chicken broth

¼ cup dry red wine

10 pitted kalamata olives, thinly sliced

2 tablespoons chopped fresh basil or ½ teaspoon dried

2 teaspoons balsamic vinegar

1. On a large sheet of wax paper, combine flour, salt, and pepper. Coat veal on both sides with seasoned flour mixture; shake to remove excess.

2. Coat a large nonstick skillet with nonstick cooking spray; heat skillet over medium-high heat. Add veal and cook 2 to 3 minutes on each side, until browned. Transfer to a plate.

3. Add peppers, scallions, and garlic to skillet; cook, stirring often, 2 minutes. Stir in tomatoes, ½ cup water, broth, wine, olives, and basil. Simmer 6 to 8 minutes, until liquid is reduced by half.

4. Stir in vinegar. Return veal to skillet. Cook 1 minute longer, or until veal is heated through.

PER SERVING Calories 209 Total Fat 6 g Saturated Fat 1 g
Cholesterol 66 mg Percentage calories from fat 25%

Veal Scallops with Caper-Mushroom Sauce

Makes 4 servings

1 pound veal scallops

¼ teaspoon salt

¼ teaspoon freshly ground black pepper

1 teaspoon olive oil

½ cup beef broth

1 pound fresh mushrooms, thinly sliced

1 cup chopped scallions

2 tablespoons chopped fresh tarragon or ¾ teaspoon dried

1 tablespoon fresh lemon juice

1 tablespoon capers, rinsed and drained

¼ cup reduced-fat sour cream

1 teaspoon Dijon mustard

1. Pound veal scallops to even thinness. Season on both sides with salt and pepper. In a large nonstick skillet, heat oil. Add veal scallops and cook 1 to 2 minutes on each side, until lightly browned. Transfer to a plate.

2. Add broth and cook, stirring to loosen brown bits from bottom of skillet. Add mushrooms, scallions, and tarragon. Cook, stirring often, 3 to 4 minutes, until mushrooms are tender. Stir in lemon juice and capers. Boil 2 to 4 minutes, until liquid is reduced by half.

3. Remove skillet from heat and slowly whisk in sour cream and mustard. Return veal to skillet. Cook, spooning sauce over veal, 1 to 2 minutes, until heated through.

PER SERVING   Calories 198   Total Fat 6 g   Saturated Fat 2 g
Cholesterol 94 mg   Percentage calories from fat 25%

Chile Barbecued Pork Chops

Makes 4 servings

1 (14½-ounce) can crushed tomatoes

1 small onion, finely chopped

2 tablespoons molasses

2 tablespoons honey

2 tablespoons fresh lime juice

2 tablespoons canned chopped green chiles

2 tablespoons chopped cilantro

2 tablespoons tomato paste

2 teaspoons Dijon mustard

½ teaspoon chili powder

¼ teaspoon ground cumin

4 lean center-cut loin pork chops, cut ½ inch thick (about 5 ounces each)

1. In a medium saucepan, combine all ingredients except pork chops. Bring to a boil, reduce heat to low, and simmer 10 minutes. Remove ½ cup sauce for basting.

2. Preheat broiler. Coat rack of a broiler pan with nonstick cooking spray.

3. Brush chops generously on both sides with sauce. Broil about 6 inches from heat 5 minutes, or until browned on top. Turn chops over and brush with more sauce. Broil 5 to 6 minutes longer, until pork is browned outside and white throughout but still moist. Boil remaining sauce for 1 to 2 minutes and pass on the side.

PER SERVING   Calories 280   Total Fat 7 g   Saturated Fat 2 g
Cholesterol 65 mg   Percentage calories from fat 22%

Spicy Kung Pao Pork

Makes 4 servings

¾ pound lean boneless pork, cut into ½-inch cubes

2 tablespoons chicken broth or dry sherry

2 tablespoons soy sauce

2 tablespoons fresh lemon juice

1 tablespoon brown sugar

2 teaspoons cornstarch

¼ teaspoon crushed hot red pepper

1 teaspoon peanut oil

3 scallions, cut into 1-inch pieces

2 garlic cloves, minced

2 cups snow peas

1 large red bell pepper, cut into 1-inch pieces

1 tablespoon unsalted dry-roasted peanuts

1. In a large bowl, combine pork cubes and chicken broth. In a small bowl, combine soy sauce, lemon juice, brown sugar, cornstarch, hot pepper, and ¼ cup water. Stir to dissolve sugar.

2. In a nonstick wok or large skillet, heat peanut oil over medium heat. Add pork with broth, scallions, and garlic; cook, stirring often, 2 minutes. Add snow peas and bell pepper; cook, stirring often, 3 to 4 minutes, until vegetables are crisp-tender and pork has no trace of pink in center.

3. Stir sauce briefly to blend cornstarch and add to wok. Cook, stirring, 1 to 2 minutes longer, until sauce thickens slightly. Sprinkle peanuts on top before serving.

PER SERVING   Calories 221   Total Fat 7 g   Saturated Fat 2 g
Cholesterol 50 mg   Percentage calories from fat 30%

Cranberry-Apple Pork Chops
Braised with Red and Green Cabbage

Makes 4 servings

4 boneless loin pork chops, cut ½ inch thick

¼ teaspoon salt

¼ teaspoon freshly ground black pepper

3 cups shredded green cabbage

3 cups shredded red cabbage

2 medium tart apples, cored and thinly sliced

1 cup apple juice

¼ cup chicken broth

3 tablespoons raspberry vinegar or cider vinegar

1 teaspoon caraway seeds

¾ cup reduced-calorie cranberry apple juice

¼ cup golden raisins

1. Season pork chops on both sides with salt and pepper. Coat a large nonstick skillet with nonstick cooking spray; heat skillet. Cook chops 2 minutes on each side, until browned. Remove from skillet and set aside.

2. Add green cabbage, red cabbage, sliced apples, apple juice, broth, vinegar, and caraway seeds to same skillet. Bring to a boil. Reduce heat to medium-low; cover and cook until cabbage is wilted, about 5 minutes. Stir in cranberry juice and raisins. Return pork to skillet. Cover and simmer 6 to 8 minutes longer, spooning sauce over chops, until pork is no longer pink in center. Serve chops with cabbage and any remaining liquid.

PER SERVING   Calories 285   Total Fat 6 g   Saturated Fat 2 g
Cholesterol 66 mg   Percentage calories from fat 19%

Spiced Lamb with Minted Couscous

Makes 4 servings

¼ cup chopped cilantro or parsley

2 tablespoons fresh lemon juice

3 garlic cloves, finely minced

1 tablespoon honey

½ teaspoon cinnamon

½ teaspoon ground cumin

⅛ teaspoon hot red pepper sauce, or to taste

¾ pound lean boneless lamb (from the leg), cut into 1-inch cubes

1 cup reduced-sodium chicken broth

½ cup tomato sauce

¼ cup chopped fresh mint

1 teaspoon grated lemon zest

1 cup quick-cooking couscous

1. In a mixing bowl, combine cilantro, lemon juice, garlic, honey, cinnamon, cumin, and hot sauce. Add lamb cubes; toss to mix well. Let marinate at room temperature 5 to 10 minutes.

2. Coat a large nonstick skillet with nonstick cooking spray; heat skillet over medium-high heat. Add lamb cubes with any remaining marinade and cook, stirring often, 6 to 8 minutes, until lamb is lightly browned and cooked to medium, or to desired doneness.

3. Meanwhile, in a medium saucepan, bring broth, tomato sauce, mint, and lemon zest to a boil. Stir in couscous. Remove saucepan from heat; cover and set aside 5 minutes.

4. To serve, fluff couscous with a fork to separate grains. Divide couscous among 4 plates. Top with lamb cubes.

PER SERVING   Calories 329   Total Fat 5 g   Saturated Fat 2 g
Cholesterol 55 mg   Percentage calories from fat 15%

Balsamic Lamb Kabobs

Makes 4 servings

¼ cup balsamic vinegar

2 tablespoons beef broth

1 tablespoon orange juice

1 tablespoon honey

2 teaspoons olive oil

2 garlic cloves, minced

½ teaspoon crushed rosemary

¼ teaspoon salt

¼ teaspoon freshly ground black pepper

¾ pound lean boneless leg of lamb, cut into 1-inch cubes

12 cherry tomatoes

1 small eggplant, cut into 1-inch cubes

1 medium red onion, cut into 1-inch chunks

1 large lemon

1. Preheat boiler or grill. In a medium bowl, combine vinegar, broth, orange juice, honey, oil, garlic, rosemary, salt, and pepper. Add lamb cubes and toss to mix well. Let marinate at room temperature 5 to 10 minutes.

2. Thread equal amounts of lamb cubes, tomatoes, eggplant, and onion on 4 metal or water-soaked bamboo skewers. Squeeze lemon juice over lamb.

3. Broil or grill skewers, turning and brushing with remaining marinade, 8 to 10 minutes, for medium rare, or until done to taste.

PER SERVING   Calories 203   Total Fat 7 g   Saturated Fat 2 g
Cholesterol 57 mg   Percentage calories from fat 30%

Seafood in a
Snap

Many fish and most shellfish are naturally light in fat and require only brief cooking times, usually 10 minutes or less. For really lean dining, stick to the paler, white-fleshed fish, such as flounder, sole, snapper, and halibut. I've included recipes for salmon and fresh tuna that still come in at or under 30 percent calories-from-fat, but keep in mind that these fish are much higher in fat and consequently in calories as well. It happens that these oilier fish are a great source of omega-3 fatty acids, so don't omit them completely, but remember to make daily total fat allowances when they are eaten.

Of course, when it comes to speed, you can't beat seafood. Both fish and shellfish should be cooked until their protein fibers are just firm and set. This takes very little time: 2 or 3 minutes for shrimp and scallops and 10 to 12 minutes for most fish. You can see the change from the soft, slightly translucent raw state to the white, firm but still moist cooked state. Many recipes will test for doneness by saying to cook until the fish turns opaque and flakes with a fork. Mussels and clams should be cooked until they open; discard any that remain closed.

The dishes in this chapter range from fairly casual Broiled Crab Cakes and Spinach-Steamed Halibut to the more elegant Snapper Veracruz, Braised Salmon with Honey and Tarragon, and Feta Shrimp with Creamy Tomatoes. All are simple to prepare and easy to serve, requiring only steamed new potatoes or rice as accompaniment.

Ginger Poached Flounder with Vegetables and Brown Rice

Makes 4 servings

This delicate dish is a meal in itself. Tender fish fillets are poached in an Asian-flavored broth along with fresh vegetables. They are served together over brown rice in a shallow bowl to be eaten like a hearty soup.

½ cup instant brown rice

1 cup reduced-sodium chicken broth

1 cup clam juice

4 thin slices fresh lemon

1 tablespoon minced fresh ginger

1 teaspoon teriyaki sauce

¼ teaspoon crushed hot red pepper

1½ cups snow peas, cut into thin strips

1 medium red bell pepper, cut into ¾-inch dice

1 medium carrot, thinly sliced

3 scallions, cut into 1-inch pieces

4 (6-ounce) flounder fillets

1. In a small saucepan, bring 1 cup water to a boil. Stir in brown rice. Cover and remove from heat. Let stand at least 5 minutes.

2. Meanwhile, in a large nonstick skillet, combine chicken broth, clam juice, lemon slices, ginger, teriyaki sauce, hot pepper, and 1¼ cups water. Bring to a boil; reduce heat to low. Add snow peas, bell pepper, carrots, and scallions. Cook 4 minutes, or until vegetables are crisp-tender.

3. Gently place flounder fillets in simmering broth. If there is not enough liquid to cover, add more water. Cover and poach 5 to 6 minutes, until fish flakes when prodded gently with a fork.

4. Divide brown rice among 4 shallow soup bowls. With a spatula, gently transfer fillets to bowls. Ladle hot broth and vegetables over fish. Serve at once.

PER SERVING   Calories 246   Total Fat 3 g   Saturated Fat 1 g
Cholesterol 82 mg   Percentage calories from fat 10%

Monkfish with Citrus and Fennel

Makes 4 servings

4 (6-ounce) monkfish fillets
1 tablespoon Pernod or 1½ teaspoons anise-flavored extract
¼ teaspoon salt
¼ teaspoon freshly ground black pepper
2 cups coarsely chopped fennel
1 medium navel orange, peeled and cut into ½-inch-thick rounds
1 cup pink grapefruit sections
½ cup chopped chives
½ cup orange-grapefruit juice

1. Preheat oven to 400 degrees F. Place monkfish in an 8-inch-square nonstick baking pan. Sprinkle with Pernod, salt, and pepper.

2. In a medium bowl, combine fennel, orange, grapefruit, chives, and orange-grapefruit juice. Spoon fennel mixture evenly over monkfish.

3. Bake 12 to 15 minutes, until fish flakes when prodded gently.

PER SERVING   Calories 199   Total Fat 3 g   Saturated Fat 0 g
Cholesterol 43 mg   Percentage calories from fat 14%

Orange Roughy with Tropical Sauce

Makes 4 servings

Many supermarkets now have whole sections devoted to fresh exotic produce. This recipe takes advantage of these new fruits. If plantains are hard to find, substitute 1 large ripe banana. I've called for whole wheat couscous here to give the dish a nuttier taste, but regular couscous is just as acceptable.

2½ cups reduced-sodium chicken broth
1 cup whole wheat couscous
½ cup chopped watercress
2 teaspoons reduced-calorie margarine
1 plantain, peeled and cut into ½-inch slices
4 (6-ounce) orange roughy fillets, cut into 1½-inch squares
1 cup cubed (½-inch) papaya
¾ cup orange-pineapple juice
¼ cup evaporated skimmed milk
1 teaspoon coconut extract
Pinch ground white pepper
1 kiwifruit, peeled and thinly sliced
2 tablespoons chopped fresh mint (optional)

1. In a medium saucepan, bring 1½ cups broth to a boil. Stir in couscous and watercress. Remove saucepan from heat. Cover and set aside.

2. In a large nonstick skillet sprayed with nonstick cooking spray, melt margarine over medium heat. Add plantains and cook 2 to 3 minutes, turning often, until golden brown. Add fish and cook, stirring often, 3 to 5 minutes, until fish looks white.

3. Stir in remaining broth, papaya cubes, orange-pineapple juice, skimmed milk, coconut extract, and white pepper. Cook 2 to 3 minutes longer, until heated through but not boiling.

4. To serve, spoon couscous onto a serving platter. Arrange fish and sauce with fruit on top. Garnish with kiwi slices and mint.

PER SERVING   Calories 527   Total Fat 14 g   Saturated Fat <1 g
Cholesterol 35 mg   Percentage calories from fat 24%

Spinach-Steamed Halibut

Makes 4 servings

Nothing too fancy, but this dish will be sure to win rave reviews from a health standpoint and certainly for fresh flavor. Serve with steamed rice.

1 cup reduced-sodium chicken broth or water

8 large spinach leaves

4 (6-ounce) halibut fillets

¼ cup nonfat Italian dressing

¼ cup chopped fresh dill or 2 teaspoons dried

1 teaspoon grated lemon zest

2 garlic cloves, minced

½ teaspoon paprika

1. Bring broth to a boil in a medium saucepan. Add spinach leaves; cook 15 seconds. Drain immediately and rinse briefly under cold running water. Place spinach leaves on a flat work surface.

2. Arrange 2 leaves so that they overlap slightly. Place a halibut fillet in the center of each leaf, folding fish in half if necessary to fit. Sprinkle equal amounts of dressing, dill, lemon zest, garlic, and paprika over each fillet. Fold bottom of spinach leaves over fillets, then fold in sides toward center, rolling to enclose.

3. Place packets on a steamer rack set 3 inches above boiling water. Cover tightly and steam 12 minutes, or until halibut is opaque throughout.

PER SERVING   Calories 205   Total Fat 4 g   Saturated Fat <1 g
Cholesterol 54 mg   Percentage calories from fat 19%

Braised Salmon with Honey and Tarragon

Makes 4 servings

1 cup instant rice

⅓ cup seasoned rice wine vinegar

2 tablespoons honey

1 teaspoon grated lemon zest

1 teaspoon olive oil

1 teaspoon Dijon mustard

1 teaspoon dried tarragon

4 (5-ounce) salmon fillets

1 lemon, cut into wedges

1. In a small saucepan, bring 2 cups of water with a pinch of salt to a boil. Stir in rice, cover pan, and remove from heat. Let stand, covered, while you prepare fish.

2. In a wide shallow bowl, combine vinegar, honey, lemon zest, oil, mustard, and tarragon. Dip salmon fillets in honey mixture, turning to coat on both sides. Leave fillets in bowl to marinate, turning once or twice, 5 to 10 minutes.

3. Coat a large nonstick skillet with nonstick cooking spray; heat over medium-high heat. Remove salmon from marinade, reserving marinade, and place fillets in skillet. Cook salmon 4 minutes. Turn fillets over and pour marinade onto fish. Cook 5 to 6 minutes longer, until fish is just opaque throughout.

4. Make a bed of rice on a serving platter. Arrange fish on top of rice. Drizzle with any juices remaining in skillet. Garnish with lemon wedges.

PER SERVING   Calories 403   Total Fat 11 g   Saturated Fat 2 g
Cholesterol 78 mg   Percentage calories from fat 24%

Baked Salmon with
Tomato Pepper Sauce

Makes 4 servings

1 teaspoon olive oil

1 small onion, chopped

2 medium tomatoes, chopped

1 (7-ounce) jar roasted red peppers, drained and coarsely
    chopped

1 tablespoon balsamic vinegar

1 teaspoon dried basil

¼ teaspoon fennel seeds, crushed

½ cup low-fat plain yogurt

Salt and freshly ground black pepper

4 (6-ounce) skinless salmon fillets

2 tablespoons chopped flat-leaf parsley

1 cup instant rice

1. Preheat oven to 350 degrees F. Coat an 8-inch-square baking pan with nonstick cooking spray.

2. In large nonstick skillet, heat oil. Add onion and cook over medium-high heat, stirring often, 2 to 3 minutes, until softened. Stir in tomatoes, roasted peppers, vinegar, basil, and fennel seeds. Simmer 5 to 7 minutes, until liquid from tomatoes evaporates. Transfer mixture to a food processor. Process until coarsely pureed. Add yogurt and puree until smooth. Season with salt and pepper to taste.

3. Place salmon fillets in prepared baking pan. Spoon equal amounts of sauce over fillets. Top each with ½ tablespoon chopped parsley. Bake 8 to 10 minutes, until fish flakes easily when tested with a fork.

4. Meanwhile, in a small saucepan, bring 2 cups water with a pinch of salt to a boil. Stir in rice, cover pan, and remove from heat. Let stand 5 minutes.

5. Make a bed of rice on a serving platter. Arrange salmon fillets on top of rice. Pour sauce over salmon and serve.

PER SERVING   Calories 445   Total Fat 13 g   Saturated Fat 2 g
Cholesterol 94 mg   Percentage calories from fat 27%

Broiled Swordfish with Green Sauce

Makes 4 servings

This multipurpose Italian-style green sauce is packed with fresh flavor from fresh herbs. It goes beautifully with the halibut here and with almost any other fish. I also like to serve it over grilled pork or even steamed vegetables.

½ cup fresh basil leaves

½ cup flat-leaf parsley leaves

3 tablespoons fresh lemon juice

2 tablespoons minced shallots

1 large hard-cooked egg white, coarsely chopped

1 tablespoon nonfat mayonnaise

1 anchovy, rinsed

⅓ cup clam juice

4 (6-ounce) swordfish steaks

½ teaspoon freshly ground black pepper

½ teaspoon garlic powder

1. Preheat broiler. Coat a broiler rack with nonstick cooking spray. In a food processor, combine basil, parsley, lemon juice, shallots, egg white, mayonnaise, and anchovy. Process until finely chopped. With machine on, gradually add clam juice. Process until sauce is smooth and thick.

2. Season swordfish on both sides with pepper and garlic powder; place on prepared rack.

3. Broil about 4 inches from heat 3 to 5 minutes on each side, until fish is browned outside and just opaque throughout. Serve swordfish with green sauce on the side.

PER SERVING   Calories 246   Total Fat 8 g   Saturated Fat 2 g
Cholesterol 58 mg   Percentage calories from fat 29%

Savory Snapper with Garlic-Lime Sauce

Makes 4 servings

2 teaspoons olive oil

4 garlic cloves, thinly sliced

3 tablespoons flour

1½ teaspoons grated lime zest

¼ teaspoon ground cumin

¼ teaspoon ground coriander

¼ teaspoon salt

¼ teaspoon freshly ground black pepper

4 (6-ounce) skinless red snapper fillets

¼ cup chicken broth

2 tablespoons fresh lime juice

1. In a large nonstick skillet, heat 1 teaspoon oil over medium heat. Add garlic and cook, stirring constantly, 1 to 2 minutes, until softened and fragrant. With a slotted spoon, remove garlic and set aside.

2. On a large sheet of wax paper, combine flour, lime zest, cumin, coriander, salt, and pepper; mix well. Dredge snapper fillets in seasoned flour, turning to coat on both sides; shake off excess.

3. Add remaining 1 teaspoon oil to skillet; heat over medium-high heat. Add snapper fillets and cook 3 to 4 minutes on each side, until fish is golden brown outside and flakes when prodded gently with a fork.

4. Add broth and lime juice to skillet; return garlic to pan. Cook 30 seconds longer, spooning sauce over fillets. Serve at once.

PER SERVING   Calories 221   Total Fat 5 g   Saturated Fat 1 g
Cholesterol 63 mg   Percentage calories from fat 20%

Snapper Veracruz

Makes 4 servings

Olives, chiles, capers, tomatoes, and herbs combine the flavors of Mexico and Spain in this classic dish. If you have the tiny nonpareil capers, leave them whole; if you're using the large ones, chop them coarsely. Serve with rice and a cucumber salad.

4 (6-ounce) skinless red snapper fillets

2 tablespoons fresh lime juice

1 teaspoon olive oil

1 medium onion, chopped

2 garlic cloves, minced

1 (28-ounce) can crushed tomatoes

1 cup reduced-sodium clam juice

1 teaspoon dried thyme

1 bay leaf

½ teaspoon dried marjoram

½ teaspoon cinnamon

Pinch ground cloves

8 pimiento-stuffed olives, chopped

2 tablespoons capers, rinsed and drained

2 pickled jalapeño peppers, seeded and thinly sliced

2 tablespoons chopped fresh parsley

1. Place fish fillets in a large glass baking dish; sprinkle with lime juice and set aside.

2. Meanwhile, in a large nonstick skillet, heat oil over medium-high heat. Add onions and garlic; cook, stirring often, 2 to 3 minutes, until softened. Stir in tomatoes, clam juice, thyme, bay leaf, marjoram, cinnamon, and cloves. Bring to a boil; reduce heat to low. Stir in olives, capers, and jalapeños. Simmer 6 to 8 minutes, until sauce thickens slightly.

3. Place fish fillets on top of sauce. Cover skillet and cook, spooning sauce over fillets several times, 5 to 6 minutes, until fish is opaque and flakes easily with a fork. Remove bay leaf and serve at once, garnished with chopped parsley.

PER SERVING   Calories 256   Total Fat 5 g   Saturated Fat 1 g
Cholesterol 63 mg   Percentage calories from fat 18%

Island Spiced Tuna

Makes 4 servings

The hot seasoning blend rubbed on these tuna steaks is typically called "jerked." It comes from the Caribbean and works equally well on grilled poultry and meats. Serve this meaty fish dish with roasted new potatoes and steamed broccoli.

1 small onion, chopped

1 small fresh hot chile pepper, seeded

2 garlic cloves

1½ teaspoons dried thyme

½ teaspoon cinnamon

¼ teaspoon allspice

¼ teaspoon salt

Pinch nutmeg

⅛ teaspoon hot red pepper sauce, or more to taste

4 (6-ounce) tuna steaks, cut about ½ inch thick

1. In a food processor, combine onion, chile pepper, garlic, thyme, cinnamon, allspice, salt, nutmeg, and hot sauce. Puree until smooth.

2. Rub spice mixture on both sides of tuna steaks. Let stand for 5 to 10 minutes.

3. Meanwhile, preheat broiler or light a hot fire in a barbecue grill. Coat broiler or grill rack with nonstick cooking spray. Broil or grill tuna 5 to 6 minutes on each side, or until browned outside and just cooked through but still moist.

PER SERVING   Calories 232   Total Fat 8 g   Saturated Fat 2 g
Cholesterol 58 mg   Percentage calories from fat 30%

Broiled Crab Cakes

Makes 4 servings

Crab cakes are a favorite of almost everyone. Here's an easy, low-fat way to make them at home. Serve with coleslaw and pickled beets.

2 cups fresh bread crumbs
½ cup egg substitute
¼ cup minced scallions
2 tablespoons chopped fresh dill
2 tablespoons chopped fresh parsley
2 teaspoons sweet pickle relish
2 teaspoons fresh lemon juice
1 teaspoon prepared white horseradish
¼ teaspoon salt
2 (7½-ounce) cans crabmeat, drained and picked over for bones
Lemon wedges

1. Preheat broiler. Coat a baking sheet with nonstick cooking spray. In a medium bowl, combine 1½ cups crumbs with egg substitute, scallions, dill, parsley, relish, lemon juice, horseradish, and salt; blend well. Add crabmeat, and mix to break up pieces of crab and to fully combine. Shape mixture into 8 small patties about ½ inch thick.

2. Place remaining ½ cup crumbs on sheet of wax paper. Coat crab cakes on both sides with crumbs. Place on prepared baking sheet. Broil about 6 inches from heat 3 to 4 minutes on each side, until golden brown. Serve hot, garnished with lemon wedges.

PER SERVING   Calories 168   Total Fat 2 g   Saturated Fat <1 g
Cholesterol 74 mg   Percentage calories from fat 12%

Steamed Lobster with Roasted Pepper Compote

Makes 4 servings

Melted butter typically accompanies lobster, but here a low-fat, savory red pepper sauce is offered instead. Serve lobsters with crusty bread and steamed asparagus.

1 (7-ounce) jar roasted red peppers, drained

3 scallions, cut into 1-inch pieces

2 garlic cloves

1 tablespoon capers, rinsed and drained

2 teaspoons red wine vinegar

1 teaspoon prepared white horseradish

1 teaspoon olive oil

4 (1-pound) live lobsters

1 large lemon, cut into wedges

1. In a food processor, combine roasted peppers, scallions, garlic, capers, vinegar, horseradish, and oil. Puree pepper compote until smooth.

2. Bring a large stockpot of water to a boil over high heat. Plunge in lobsters and cook 12 minutes; lobsters are done when they turn bright red and meat is opaque throughout.

3. Remove lobsters with tongs. Carefully cut open underside with kitchen scissors from tail to head. With a teaspoon, scoop out and discard sand sac from head. Set lobsters on individual plates and serve with pepper compote and lemon wedges.

PER SERVING   Calories 139   Total Fat 2 g   Saturated Fat <1 g
Cholesterol 72 mg   Percentage calories from fat 12%

Steamed Mussels with Bell Peppers

Makes 4 servings

1 tablespoon reduced-calorie margarine

1 medium red bell pepper, finely diced

1 medium green bell pepper, finely diced

1 small onion, chopped

2 garlic cloves, minced

½ teaspoon salt-free lemon-herb seasoning blend

½ teaspoon dried basil

1 cup reduced-sodium chicken broth

⅓ cup reduced-sodium clam juice

2 teaspoons balsamic vinegar

4 dozen mussels, scrubbed and debearded

⅓ cup dry-pack sun-dried tomato bits

¼ cup chopped fresh parsley (optional)

1. In a large nonstick skillet, melt margarine over medium-high heat. Add bell peppers, onion, garlic, herb seasoning, and basil; cook, stirring often, 4 to 5 minutes, until vegetables are softened. Stir in broth, clam juice, and vinegar. Bring to a boil; reduce heat to medium.

2. Add mussels and sun-dried tomatoes. Cover skillet and cook 4 to 6 minutes, until mussels open. Discard any mussels that do not open.

3. To serve, divide mussels among 4 shallow bowls. Pour broth and vegetables over mussels. Garnish with parsley and serve at once.

PER SERVING   Calories 150   Total Fat 4 g   Saturated Fat 1 g
Cholesterol 27 mg   Percentage calories from fat 23%

Scallop Scampi

Makes 4 servings

Scampi, which usually refers to shrimp, is traditionally made with butter, oil, garlic, and lemon juice. This recipe broils scallops in the same type of sauce, but to reduce fat intake it employs butter-flavored sprinkles, which you'll find in the spice aisle of your supermarket. Serve with rice or angel hair pasta and steamed zucchini.

⅓ cup butter-flavored sprinkles

¼ cup minced shallots

3 garlic cloves, crushed

2 tablespoons fresh lemon juice

1 teaspoon grated lemon zest

1 teaspoon olive oil

¼ teaspoon freshly ground black pepper

1 pound bay or sea scallops

¼ teaspoon paprika

1. Preheat broiler. Coat a shallow baking dish with nonstick cooking spray. Add sprinkles, shallots, garlic, lemon juice, lemon zest, olive oil, and pepper; stir to combine. Add scallops; toss to mix well.

2. Arrange scallops in a single layer. Sprinkle paprika on top.

3. Broil scallops about 4 inches from heat 3 minutes. Turn over and broil 1 to 2 minutes longer, until scallops are opaque throughout.

PER SERVING   Calories 146   Total Fat 2 g   Saturated Fat <1 g
Cholesterol 39 mg   Percentage calories from fat 13%

Shrimp Burritos

Makes 4 servings

Flour tortillas enclose spicy shrimp tossed with cooked fresh tomatoes, avocado, chiles, and cilantro. Serve with Mexican rice or just a tossed salad.

4 large (10-inch) flour tortillas
1 pound cooked peeled medium shrimp
2 medium tomatoes, coarsely chopped
1 cup coarsely chopped arugula or romaine lettuce
½ medium red onion, chopped
½ cup diced (½-inch) avocado
¼ cup canned chopped green chiles
2 tablespoons chopped fresh cilantro
2 tablespoons red wine vinegar
½ teaspoon ground cumin
½ teaspoon chili powder
½ cup fat-free refried beans
¼ cup nonfat sour cream

1. Preheat oven to 325 degrees F. Wrap tortillas in foil and place in oven to warm.

2. In a medium bowl, combine all remaining ingredients except beans and sour cream; toss to mix well. Set aside to marinate for 5 to 10 minutes.

3. To assemble, remove tortillas from oven. Spread 2 tablespoons refried beans over each tortilla to within 1 inch of edge. Spoon equal amounts of shrimp mixture down center of tortillas. Top each with 1 tablespoon sour cream. Fold in sides and roll up to enclose filling. Serve at once.

PER SERVING   Calories 328   Total Fat 8 g   Saturated Fat 1 g
Cholesterol 73 mg   Percentage calories from fat 22%

Feta Shrimp with Creamy Tomatoes

Makes 4 servings

To make the most of this saucy dish, make sure to serve over rice or pasta.

1 teaspoon olive oil

1 green bell pepper, chopped

1 red bell pepper, chopped

1 cup chopped scallions

1 small fresh hot pepper, seeded and finely chopped

½ cup chopped fresh basil

½ teaspoon dried oregano

½ teaspoon dried thyme

1 (14½-ounce) can diced tomatoes, drained

½ teaspoon brown sugar

24 cleaned peeled medium shrimp

3 tablespoons crumbled feta cheese, preferably herb-flavored

2 tablespoons skim milk

1. In a large nonstick skillet, heat oil over medium-high heat. Add bell peppers, scallions, and hot pepper. Cook, stirring often, 2 to 4 minutes, until bell peppers are softened. Stir in basil, oregano, and thyme; cook 1 minute.

2. Reduce heat to medium. Stir in tomatoes and sugar. Simmer about 5 minutes, until sauce thickens slightly. Add shrimp and cook, stirring, until they are pink and loosely curled, 1 to 2 minutes.

3. Stir in cheese and milk. Cook 2 minutes longer, just until cheese starts to melt.

PER SERVING   Calories 130   Total Fat 4 g   Saturated Fat 1 g
Cholesterol 78 mg   Percentage calories from fat 25%

Meatless Main Courses in Minutes

Even those of us who are not full-time vegetarians can appreciate the pleasures and health benefits of an occasional meat-free meal. Contemporary nutritional studies suggest there are benefits to eating less meat and more bean, whole grain, and vegetable dishes. That's because saturated fats and cholesterol, which seem to be culprits in heart disease and some forms of cancer, are found almost exclusively in animal products. Meatless eating has opened a doorway to a whole new world of enticing recipes.

Vegetarian cooking need not entail unfamiliar foods and endless trips to health food stores. This chapter was designed to ease vegetarian recipes into your diet and at the same time to excite you about a whole new way of eating. To accomplish this goal, I made sure that all the ingredients used here can be found in most supermarkets. Tofu does appear in a couple of recipes, but these days you'll find it packaged, in the refrigerated section of your supermarket, not far from the yogurt and cottage cheese.

Most of these dishes are much more familiar, tastes I'm sure your whole family will enjoy: Ratatouille and Bean-Stuffed Potatoes, Brown Rice Paella, and Tortellini Casserole with Eggplant and Cheese, to name just a few. Hopefully they prove that vegetarian eating, which is a great way to lower total saturated fat and cholesterol, need not be a challenging chore.

Barbecued Bean Stew

Makes 4 servings

2 teaspoons olive oil

1 cup chopped scallions

1 medium carrot, chopped

1 medium celery rib, chopped

2 garlic cloves, minced

1 (15-ounce) can black beans, rinsed and drained

1 (15-ounce) can red kidney beans, rinsed and drained

1 cup drained canned black-eyed peas

1 cup corn kernels, canned or thawed frozen

1 (15-ounce) can stewed tomatoes

2 tablespoons reduced-calorie barbecue sauce

1 tablespoon reduced-calorie maple syrup

2 teaspoons red wine vinegar

½ teaspoon chili powder

2 ounces baked tortilla chips (approximately 26 chips)

¼ cup nonfat sour cream

1. In a large heavy saucepan, heat oil over medium heat. Add scallions, carrots, celery, and garlic. Cook, stirring often, 5 minutes.

2. Stir in black and red beans, black-eyed peas, corn, stewed tomatoes, barbecue sauce, maple syrup. vinegar, and chili powder. Simmer 10 to 12 minutes, stirring often, until stew thickens slightly.

3. To serve, divide stew evenly among 4 bowls. Crush equal amounts of tortilla chips on top of stew. Top each with 1 tablespoon sour cream.

PER SERVING   Calories 371   Total Fat 7 g   Saturated Fat 1 g
Cholesterol 0 mg   Percentage calories from fat 16%

Mushroom and Roasted Red Pepper Pizza

Makes 4 servings

10 ounces mushrooms, thinly sliced

1 (7-ounce) jar roasted red peppers, drained and cut into strips

6 cups coarsely chopped fresh spinach

1 cup coarsely chopped marinated artichoke hearts

2 teaspoons balsamic vinegar

¼ teaspoon crushed rosemary

1 (12-inch) Italian bread shell, such as Boboli

½ cup tomato sauce

1½ ounces crumbled goat cheese or feta

1. Preheat oven to 400 degrees F. Coat a large nonstick skillet with nonstick cooking spray; heat over medium-high heat. Add mushrooms and cook, stirring often, 2 minutes. Stir in peppers; cook 1 minute longer. Add spinach, artichokes, vinegar, and rosemary. Cook, stirring often, 2 to 3 minutes, until spinach is wilted and tender but still bright green.

2. Place bread shell on a large baking sheet. Spread tomato sauce over bread. Cover with mushroom-spinach mixture. Sprinkle goat cheese on top.

3. Bake 10 to 12 minutes, until bread is golden brown and cheese begins to melt.

PER SERVING   Calories 466   Total Fat 14 g   Saturated Fat 5 g
Cholesterol 18 mg   Percentage calories from fat 27%

Curried Beans over Couscous

Makes 4 servings

*C*urry *is a great seasoning for all kinds of dishes, including vegetarian. Its potent flavor adds pizzazz to almost any ingredient it is paired with, creating taste satisfaction that is sometimes missed in meatless meals. Three different legumes—black beans, chickpeas, and black-eyed peas provide extra interest of color and texture here.*

1 cup reduced-sodium chicken broth

½ cup orange juice

1 teaspoon grated lime zest

1 cup quick-cooking couscous

2 teaspoons peanut oil

1 cup chopped scallions

1 tablespoon finely chopped fresh ginger

2 garlic cloves, minced

1½ teaspoons curry powder

3 medium tomatoes, coarsely chopped

2 tablespoons chopped fresh cilantro or parsley

1 (15-ounce) can black beans, rinsed and drained

1 (15-ounce) can chickpeas, rinsed and drained

½ cup drained canned black-eyed peas

1 tablespoon fresh lime juice

1. In a medium saucepan, bring broth, orange juice, and lime zest to a boil. Stir in couscous. Remove saucepan from heat. Cover and set aside.

2. In large nonstick skillet, heat oil over medium heat. Add scallions, ginger, garlic, and curry powder. Cook, stirring often, 2 minutes. Add tomatoes and cilantro, raise heat to high, and cook 2 minutes, or until mixture thickens slightly.

3. Reduce heat to medium-low. Stir in black beans, chickpeas, black-eyed peas, and lime juice. Cover skillet and simmer 5 minutes. To serve, divide couscous among 4 plates. Top with equal amounts of bean curry.

PER SERVING   Calories 410   Total Fat 5 g   Saturated Fat 1 g
Cholesterol 0 mg   Percentage calories from fat 12%

Kasha with White Beans and Bow Ties

Makes 4 servings

Kasha is another word for buckwheat groats. They are classically paired with bow tie pasta. Here I've added beans as well to turn this into a hearty main dish.

1 cup bow tie pasta

1 cup kasha

2 large egg whites, lightly beaten

2 teaspoons olive oil

1 medium onion, thinly sliced and separated into rings

10 ounces mushrooms, thinly sliced

2 cups reduced-sodium chicken broth

½ teaspoon dried thyme

¼ teaspoon salt

¼ teaspoon freshly ground black pepper

1 teaspoon sugar

1 (15-ounce) can small white beans, rinsed and drained

2 tablespoons chopped fresh parsley

1. In a medium saucepan of boiling salted water, cook pasta 10 to 12 minutes, until tender but still firm. Drain into a colander.

2. Meanwhile, in a medium bowl, combine kasha and egg whites. Stir until grains of kasha are thoroughly coated with egg white.

3. In a large nonstick skillet, heat oil over medium-high heat. Add onions and mushrooms; cook, stirring occasionally, 3 minutes. Stir in ¼ cup broth, thyme, salt, and pepper. Cook, stirring often, 5 to 6 minutes longer, until vegetables are tender.

4. Stir kasha and sugar into skillet. Cook, stirring often, 2 to 4 minutes, until kasha begins to stick to skillet and gives off a nutty aroma. Stir in the remaining 1¾ cups broth. Bring to a boil; reduce heat to low.

5. Add beans, cooked pasta, and parsley. Cover and simmer 8 to 10 minutes longer, until kasha is tender and most of liquid has been absorbed.

PER SERVING   Calories 322   Total Fat 5g   Saturated Fat 1g
Cholesterol 9mg   Percentage calories from fat 13%

Ratatouille and
Bean-Stuffed Potatoes

Makes 4 servings

*W*ant *baked potatoes in nothing flat? Cook them in the microwave. On average, a large baking potato will take 4 to 6 minutes on high power. More potatoes take proportionally more time, but 4 whoppers will still take less time than it takes to preheat your conventional oven. Here plenty of vegetables and a bolstering helping of beans turn this into a hearty vegetarian main course.*

4 medium-large baking potatoes (about ½ pound each)

2 teaspoons olive oil

1 red bell pepper, chopped

½ cup chopped red onion

3 garlic cloves, minced

1 small eggplant (about ¾ pound)

2 small zucchini, thinly sliced

1 (14½-ounce) can pasta-ready tomatoes

1 tablespoon tomato paste

2 teaspoons rinsed, drained capers

2 tablespoons chopped fresh basil or ¾ teaspoon dried

¼ teaspoon finely crushed rosemary

¼ teaspoon freshly ground black pepper

1 (15-ounce) can small white beans, rinsed and drained

1. Poke potatoes in several places. Arrange in a spoke pattern on a double thickness of microwave-safe paper towel and microwave on high 5 minutes. Turn over and microwave 3 to 5 minutes longer, until tender.

2. In a large nonstick skillet, heat oil over medium-high heat. Add bell pepper, red onion, and garlic. Cook, stirring often, 2 to 3 minutes, until softened. Stir in eggplant and zucchini and cook, stirring often, 2 minutes.

3. Add tomatoes, tomato paste, capers, basil, rosemary, and black pepper. Bring to a boil; reduce heat to low, cover, and simmer 10 minutes, stirring occasionally. Stir in beans and cook 1 to 2 minutes longer, until heated through.

4. To serve, split potatoes down center and fluff each side with a fork. Spoon equal amounts of ratatouille over potatoes. Serve while hot.

PER SERVING   Calories 336   Total Fat 3 g   Saturated Fat <1 g
Cholesterol 0 mg   Percentage calories from fat 8%

Spinach and Eggplant–Stuffed Crepes

Makes 4 servings

The basic recipe for crepes in step 1 can be used to enclose many different fillings, from main dishes to desserts. Whole wheat flour gives the crepes a nutty taste that works well with the spinach-and-eggplant filling. This makes a lovely light lunch. To serve as a main course at dinner, you may want to double the recipe.

2 tablespoons whole wheat flour

½ cup egg substitute

2 tablespoons low-fat milk

½ teaspoon salt

2 teaspoons olive oil

1 small onion, chopped

2 garlic cloves, minced

1½ cups diced (½-inch) eggplant

1 medium tomato, chopped

¼ cup tomato sauce

½ teaspoon dried basil

½ teaspoon dried oregano

¼ teaspoon cinnamon

1 (10-ounce) box frozen chopped spinach, thawed and
      squeezed dry

¼ cup shredded nonfat mozzarella cheese

1. In a small bowl, whisk together flour, egg substitute, milk, ¼ teaspoon salt, and 2 tablespoons water until well blended. Set crepe batter aside.

2. In a large nonstick skillet, heat 1 teaspoon oil over medium-high heat. Add onion and garlic and cook, stirring often, 2 to 3 minutes, until softened. Add eggplant and cook 4 to 5 minutes, until eggplant is golden. Stir in tomatoes, tomato sauce, basil, oregano, cinnamon, and remaining ¼ teaspoon salt and cook 2 minutes. Stir in spinach and cook 5 to 7 minutes, stirring often, to blend flavors.

3. While vegetables are simmering, in a small (6- to 7-inch) nonstick skillet, heat remaining 1 teaspoon oil. Add one-fourth of batter to skillet; tilt to cover bottom of pan evenly. Cook 1 minute, until lightly browned on bottom. Flip crepe over and cook 30 seconds longer. Remove to a plate and cover to keep warm. Repeat to make 3 more crepes.

4. To serve, place equal amounts of spinach-and-eggplant filling down center of each crepe. Sprinkle each with 1 tablespoon cheese. Fold in sides to enclose filling. Serve at once.

PER SERVING   Calories 112   Total Fat 3 g   Saturated Fat 1 g
Cholesterol 2 mg   Percentage calories from fat 22%

Brown Rice Paella

Makes 4 servings

Now you can make an even more nutritious version of this traditional Spanish dish in nothing flat and keep all the flavor by using quick-cooking brown rice. Just a pinch of saffron is needed to impart its wonderful color and taste.

1 teaspoon olive oil

2 green bell peppers, cut into thin strips

2 small yellow squash, coarsely chopped

1 medium red onion, chopped

2 garlic cloves, minced

3 cups canned crushed tomatoes

1 (15-ounce) can chickpeas, drained

1 (10-ounce) package frozen lima beans, thawed

1 cup Mexican-style corn

1½ cups tomato juice

1½ cups vegetable broth

1 teaspoon dried thyme

½ teaspoon salt

⅛ teaspoon turmeric

Pinch saffron threads or ⅛ teaspoon ground saffron

3 cups instant brown rice

2 tablespoons chopped fresh parsley

1. In a large nonstick skillet or flameproof casserole, heat oil over medium-high heat. Add bell peppers, squash, red onion, and garlic. Cook, stirring often, 4 to 5 minutes, until vegetables are tender.

2. Stir in tomatoes, chickpeas, lima beans, and corn. Bring to a boil. Reduce heat to low and simmer 2 to 3 minutes, until liquid from tomatoes evaporates.

3. Stir in tomato juice, broth, thyme, salt, turmeric, and saffron. Bring to a boil. Stir in rice and remove skillet from heat. Cover and set aside 5 to 7 minutes, until liquid is absorbed. Fluff with a fork, garnish with parsley, and serve.

PER SERVING   Calories 537   Total Fat 7 g   Saturated Fat <1 g
Cholesterol 0 mg   Percentage calories from fat 10%

Szechuan Spaghetti Squash Stir-Fry

Makes 4 servings

Spaghetti squash offers a great way to add lots of bulk to recipes without adding lots of calories. The strands work well topped with sauces or, in this case, with plenty of vegetables in a hot and spicy stir-fry.

1 medium spaghetti squash (about 2 pounds)

½ cup chicken broth

2 tablespoons orange juice

1 tablespoon soy sauce

1 teaspoon cornstarch

¼ to ½ teaspoon crushed hot red pepper, or to taste

1 teaspoon Asian sesame oil

4 ounces firm tofu, well drained and cut into ¾-inch cubes

2 small yellow squash, coarsely chopped

1 cup shredded red cabbage

1 cup shredded napa (Chinese) or green cabbage

½ cup chopped scallions

1 cup snow peas, cut into thin strips (about 2½ ounces)

2 teaspoons toasted sesame seeds

1. Pierce spaghetti squash several times with a fork. Microwave on high 5 minutes. Turn squash over and microwave 5 minutes longer, or until tender. Let cool slightly; then cut squash lengthwise in half. Remove and discard seeds. Separate squash into strands with a fork.

2. In a small bowl, combine broth, orange juice, soy sauce, cornstarch, and hot pepper. Stir to mix well. Set sauce aside.

3. In a nonstick wok or large skillet, heat oil over high heat. Add tofu and yellow squash. Stir-fry 3 to 4 minutes, until tofu is golden. Add red cabbage, napa cabbage, scallions, snow peas, and spaghetti squash. Stir-fry 5 to 7 minutes, until cabbage is crisp-tender.

4. Give sauce a stir to blend cornstarch and add to wok. Cook, stirring, 1 minute, or until sauce thickens slightly. Sprinkle sesame seeds on top and serve.

PER SERVING   Calories 164   Total Fat 6 g   Saturated Fat 1 g
Cholesterol 0 mg   Percentage calories from fat 30%

Cheesy Stuffed Tomatoes with Crispy Topping

Makes 4 servings

1 ½ cups instant brown rice

4 large ripe tomatoes

1 (10-ounce) box frozen peas, thawed

¼ cup nonfat Caesar salad dressing

¼ cup chopped fresh basil or ½ teaspoon dried mixed with 2
        tablespoons chopped parsley

2 ounces crumbled blue cheese

¼ teaspoon salt

¼ teaspoon freshly ground black pepper

2 tablespoons grated Parmesan cheese

2 tablespoons seasoned dry bread crumbs

¼ teaspoon paprika

1. In a small saucepan, bring 1½ cups lightly salted water to a boil. Stir in brown rice, cover, and remove from heat. Let stand at least 5 minutes.

2. Meanwhile, slice tomatoes in half horizontally. With a teaspoon, scoop out pulp and coarsely chop. Place chopped tomatoes in a large bowl. Set tomato shells upside down on paper towels to drain.

3. Preheat broiler. Coat an 11 by 7-inch nonstick baking pan with nonstick cooking spray. Add brown rice, peas, salad dressing, basil, blue cheese, salt, and black pepper to chopped tomatoes in bowl. Toss to mix well.

4. Place tomatoes, cut sides up, in prepared baking pan. Stuff tomatoes with equal amounts of tomato-rice filling. Toss together Parmesan cheese, bread crumbs, and paprika; sprinkle ½ tablespoon over top of each stuffed tomato half.

5. Broil 6 inches from heat 3 to 5 minutes, until crumbs begin to brown. Serve at room temperature. (If you prefer to serve these hot, bake them in a 350 degree F. oven for 12 to 15 minutes.) Serve 2 halves per person.

PER SERVING   Calories 295   Total Fat 7 g   Saturated Fat 3g
Cholesterol 13 mg   Percentage calories from fat 21%

Tortellini Casserole with Eggplant and Cheese

Makes 4 servings

*F*resh *tortellini can be found in the refrigerated section of your supermarket. Instead of baking the casserole, it's given a few quick minutes under the broiler to produce a creamy, melted cheese topping.*

1 (9-ounce) package fresh cheese tortellini

1 teaspoon olive oil

1 medium-small eggplant, cut into 1-inch cubes

1 medium green bell pepper, cut into ½-inch dice

1 small onion, chopped

1 medium carrot, chopped

1 medium celery rib, chopped

1 (14½-ounce) can stewed tomatoes, juices reserved

1 (8-ounce) can tomato sauce

1 teaspoon red wine vinegar

½ teaspoon fennel seeds, crushed

½ teaspoon dried basil

½ cup shredded reduced-fat mozzarella cheese

1 tablespoon seasoned dry bread crumbs

1 tablespoon grated Parmesan cheese

1. In a large pot of boiling water, cook tortellini 6 to 8 minutes, until tender but still firm. Drain gently into a colander.

2. Meanwhile, in a large nonstick skillet, heat oil over medium-high heat. Add eggplant, bell pepper, onion, carrot, and celery. Cook, stirring often, 6 to 7 minutes, until vegetables are tender.

3. Stir in stewed tomatoes with their juices, tomato sauce, vinegar, fennel seeds, and basil. Bring to a boil, reduce heat to medium-low, and simmer 5 to 6 minutes, until sauce thickens slightly.

4. Preheat broiler. Coat a 12-inch oval gratin or flameproof baking dish with nonstick cooking spray. Spoon half of eggplant mixture into prepared baking dish; spread to make an even layer. Top with half of tortellini. Repeat with remaining eggplant and tortellini. Sprinkle mozzarella, bread crumbs, and Parmesan cheese evenly over top.

5. Broil 6 to 8 inches from heat 3 to 4 minutes, until cheese melts and casserole is heated through.

PER SERVING   Calories 334   Total Fat 8 g   Saturated Fat 3 g
Cholesterol 32 mg   Percentage calories from fat 22%

Vegetable-Cheese Sandwiches with Chutney Dressing

Makes 4 servings

These open-face sandwiches are perfect for hectic weeknight schedules. The vegetables and chutney sauce can be made ahead of time and refrigerated until you're ready to use them.

½ cup nonfat plain yogurt

2 tablespoons nonfat mayonnaise

1 tablespoon mango chutney

2 teaspoons lime juice

1 teaspoon honey

¼ teaspoon curry powder

2 teaspoons olive oil

1 red bell pepper, cut into thin slices

1 green bell pepper, cut into thin slices

1 medium red onion, thinly sliced and separated into rings

8 slices reduced-calorie whole grain bread

4 ounces reduced-calorie Jarlsberg cheese, thinly sliced

1 medium tomato, thinly sliced

1. In a small bowl, combine yogurt, mayonnaise, chutney, lime juice, honey, and curry powder. Mix well. Cover and refrigerate chutney sauce until serving time.

2. In a large nonstick skillet, heat oil over medium-high heat. Add bell peppers and red onion. Cook, stirring often, 6 to 8 minutes, until vegetables are very soft.

3. Preheat broiler. Place bread slices on a large baking sheet. Spread 2 tablespoons chutney sauce over each slice. Top with equal amounts of peppers and onion, cheese, and tomatoes. Broil sandwiches about 4 inches from heat 2 to 3 minutes, until cheese is melted and bubbly.

PER SERVING   Calories 262   Total Fat 8 g   Saturated Fat 3 g
Cholesterol 16 mg   Percentage calories from fat 25%

Vegetarian Bolognese Sauce

Makes 4 servings

Here I've taken a classic sauce and reproduced its texture and general flavor without the meat. I have purposely left the serving suggestion up to you. This hearty sauce is typically married with pasta; however, I like it just as well over polenta or a steamed grain.

12 dry-pack sun-dried tomato halves

1 tablespoon reduced-calorie margarine

1 cup finely chopped fennel

1 small onion, finely chopped

1 medium carrot, finely chopped

½ cup finely chopped zucchini

2 large tomatoes, coarsely chopped, or 1 (14½-ounce) can diced
tomatoes, drained

⅔ cup chicken broth

⅔ cup evaporated skimmed milk

¼ teaspoon salt

¼ teaspoon freshly ground black pepper

⅛ teaspoon nutmeg

1 cup thawed frozen peas

1 tablespoon grated Parmesan cheese

1. Place dried tomatoes in a small heatproof bowl. Cover with boiling water and let stand 5 minutes.

2. Meanwhile, in a large nonstick skillet, melt margarine over medium-high heat. Add fennel, onion, carrots, and zucchini; cook, stirring often, until vegetables are softened, about 5 minutes.

3. Drain dried tomatoes, reserving ¼ cup liquid. Add dried tomatoes, fresh tomatoes, and reserved liquid to skillet. Cook, stirring constantly, 3 to 4 minutes, until liquid evaporates.

4. Stir in broth, evaporated milk, salt, pepper, and nutmeg. Reduce heat to very low and simmer, stirring occasionally, 6 to 8 minutes. Do not let sauce come to a boil, or it may curdle. Stir in peas and cheese; cook 1 minute longer, until peas are heated through.

PER SERVING   Calories 152   Total Fat 3 g   Saturated Fat 1 g
Cholesterol 3 mg   Percentage calories from fat 15%

Fresh Vegetable Tostadas

Makes 4 servings

4 large (10-inch) flour tortillas

1 (15-ounce) can chickpeas, rinsed and drained

¼ cup nonfat cottage cheese

2 tablespoons nonfat plain yogurt

1 tablespoon reduced-fat peanut butter

1 tablespoon fresh lemon juice

2 to 3 drops hot red pepper sauce, or more to taste

2½ cups shredded red leaf or romaine lettuce

2 medium tomatoes, cut into ½-inch dice

1 cup Mexican-style canned corn

½ cup diced avocado

½ cup salsa

¼ cup nonfat sour cream

1. Preheat oven to 350 degrees F. Place tortillas on a large baking sheet. Bake 4 minutes on each side, or until crisp and golden. Remove from oven and set aside.

2. Meanwhile, in a food processor, combine chickpeas, cottage cheese, yogurt, peanut butter, lemon juice, and hot sauce. Puree until smooth. Set chickpea puree aside.

3. In a large bowl, combine lettuce, tomatoes, corn, avocado, and salsa. Toss to mix salad well.

4. To assemble tostadas, spread one-fourth of chickpea puree over each tortilla. Place equal amounts of salad on top and dollop 1 tablespoon sour cream on each.

PER SERVING   Calories 409   Total Fat 11 g   Saturated Fat 2 g
Cholesterol 1 mg   Percentage calories from fat 23%

One-Dish Dinners
on Demand

Who doesn't want to free up their weekday schedule and still pull out a tasty home-cooked meal at dinnertime? But as they say, easier said than done. What I call "one-dish dinners" are meals that come to the table all in one pot and that contain your meat (or other source of protein), starch, and vegetables all in one place. These quick and easy dinners provide one way to try and feed your family while you play beat the clock.

Some of the recipes in this chapter, such as Turkey Shepherd's Pie, can be completely prepared the night before and just heated through the next day. Others, like Supper Salad or Chicken Ratatouille, are good at room temperature or cold. And many, such as Corn Chili with Black Beans or Ham and Egg Fried Rice, come together in minutes. One dish means less hassle, less mess, and less time spent cleaning up. Even the ever-popular pizza falls into this category.

While all these one-dish dinners provide a satisfying main course, some would do well with a tossed salad on the side, and a basket of good bread is often welcome. On hectic nights when time is at a premium, serve fresh fruit or a no-fat sorbet for dessert. Learning that a home-cooked meal can be ready in minutes with low fat and little cleanup can relieve a lot of pressure for the weekday cook. Take it from one who knows.

Creamy Broccoli Chicken Breasts

Makes 4 servings

1 cup small pasta shells

1 tablespoon reduced-calorie margarine

1 small onion, chopped

1 medium celery rib, chopped

4 chicken cutlets (about 3 ounces each)

½ teaspoon garlic salt

1 (10-ounce) package frozen chopped broccoli, thawed

1 cup skim milk

12 dry-pack sun-dried tomato halves

¼ cup grated Parmesan cheese

1 teaspoon lemon juice

⅛ teaspoon ground white pepper

1. Fill a large flameproof casserole with salted water and bring to a boil. Add pasta shells and cook 10 to 12 minutes, until tender but still firm. Drain into a colander, rinse briefly under cold running water, and drain well.

2. In same casserole, melt margarine over medium heat. Add onion and celery and cook 3 to 4 minutes, until softened but not browned. Season chicken with garlic salt and add to skillet. Cook 3 to 4 minutes on each side, until golden. Remove chicken to serving plates and keep warm.

3. In same skillet add broccoli. Stir in milk, tomatoes, and Parmesan; cook, stirring often, 4 to 5 minutes, until liquid reduces slightly. Stir in shells, lemon juice, and pepper; cook 1 minute longer, until heated through.

4. To serve, spoon sauce evenly over chicken breasts.

PER SERVING   Calories 302   Total Fat 6 g   Saturated Fat 2 g
Cholesterol 56 mg   Percentage calories from fat 16%

Chicken Ratatouille

Makes 4 servings

This twist on the classic adds leftover cooked chicken to the vegetable mélange, making it a meal in a pot.

2 teaspoons olive oil
1 medium eggplant (about 1 pound), cut into 1-inch dice
1 medium red onion, chopped
2 garlic cloves, minced
4 cups chopped zucchini
1 medium green bell pepper, chopped
1 (28-ounce) can diced tomatoes, juices reserved
2 tablespoons tomato paste
2 tablespoons chopped fresh basil or ½ teaspoon dried
½ teaspoon dried oregano
¼ teaspoon crushed hot red pepper
½ pound cooked chicken, cut into ½-inch dice (1⅓ cups)
Salt and freshly ground black pepper

1. In a large nonstick skillet, heat oil over medium-high heat. Add eggplant, red onion, and garlic. Cook, stirring often, 3 to 4 minutes, until onion is softened. Add zucchini and bell pepper and cook 1 to 2 minutes.

2. Stir in tomatoes with their juices, tomato paste, basil, oregano, and hot pepper. Bring to a boil, reduce heat to medium-low, and cook 10 to 12 minutes, until liquid thickens and vegetables are tender.

3. Stir in chicken. Simmer 2 minutes. Season with salt and black pepper to taste. Serve hot, at room temperature, or chilled.

PER SERVING   Calories 210   Total Fat 4 g   Saturated Fat 1 g
Cholesterol 41 mg   Percentage calories from fat 16%

Turkey Shepherd's Pie

Makes 4 servings

This hearty one-pot dish is lightened up by using ground turkey. If you prefer to use fresh potatoes in step 1, boil 1½ pounds of quartered peeled potatoes until tender, then mash before mixing in margarine and skim milk.

4 cups instant mashed potatoes
1 tablespoon reduced-calorie margarine
½ cup skim milk
Salt
1 teaspoon olive oil
1 pound ground turkey
1 large onion, chopped
1 (10-ounce) package thinly sliced mushrooms
1½ tablespoons flour
1 (15-ounce) can mixed vegetables, drained
1 cup reduced-sodium chicken broth
2 teaspoons Worcestershire sauce

1. Preheat oven to 350 degrees F. Coat a 9-inch pie plate with non-stick cooking spray. In a medium saucepan, bring 1½ cups water to a boil. Remove from the heat and stir in the potatoes. Add the margarine and mix until melted. Stir in the milk. Season with salt to taste.

2. In a large nonstick skillet, heat oil over medium heat. Add ground turkey and onion. Cook, stirring, until turkey is no longer pink, 6 to 8 minutes.

3. Stir in mushrooms and cook until they begin to soften, 2 to 3 minutes. Sprinkle on flour and cook, stirring, 1 minute. Stir in vegetables, broth, and Worcestershire. Cook, stirring to blend flour, 5 to 6 minutes, until sauce thickens slightly. Pour mixture into prepared pie plate.

4. Spread mashed potatoes evenly over turkey mixture. Bake 25 to 30 minutes, until potatoes are golden.

PER SERVING   Calories 447   Total Fat 12 g   Saturated Fat 3 g
Cholesterol 83 mg   Percentage calories from fat 24%

Skillet Pasta and Beef

Makes 4 servings

Thinly sliced beef and already cooked pasta make this dish a quick one-dish favorite. Broccoli or asparagus can be substituted for the zucchini.

1 teaspoon olive oil
2 cups coarsely chopped zucchini
1 cup chopped onion
12 ounces sirloin steak, thinly sliced
1½ cups pasta-ready tomatoes
½ cup reduced-sodium beef broth
4 cups cooked pasta shells
½ cup chopped roasted red pepper
½ cup drained canned corn
2 tablespoons chopped fresh basil
2 tablespoons grated Parmesan cheese

1. In a large nonstick skillet, heat oil. Add zucchini and onion; cook, stirring often, 4 to 5 minutes, until tender. Add steak; cook 1 to 2 minutes, until beef is no longer pink.

2. Stir remaining ingredients into skillet; bring to a boil. Reduce heat to low; simmer 5 to 7 minutes longer, until sauce thickens slightly and pasta is heated through.

Turkey Lo Mein

Makes 4 servings

I've updated the traditional Chinese noodle dish by greatly reducing the amount of oil used to stir-fry, employing just a little lean turkey in place of fattier meats, and packing the dish with plenty of fresh vegetables.

2 teaspoons peanut oil
½ pound mushrooms, thinly sliced
1 red bell pepper, cut into strips
1 cup shredded cabbage
¼ pound snow peas
½ cup bean sprouts
½ pound thinly sliced turkey breast, cut into strips
½ cup chicken broth
1 tablespoon soy sauce
2 teaspoons cornstarch
½ teaspoon Chinese five-spice powder
2 cups cooked Chinese noodles or spaghetti

1. In a nonstick wok or large skillet, heat oil. Add mushrooms and bell pepper. Cook, stirring often, 3 to 4 minutes, until pepper is crisp-tender. Add cabbage, snow peas, and bean sprouts; cook 2 minutes longer. Remove vegetables from skillet.

2. In a medium bowl, toss turkey strips with 3 tablespoons of broth, soy sauce, cornstarch, and five-spice powder. Add to wok and cook over medium-high heat, stirring often, 3 to 4 minutes, until turkey is no longer pink.

3. Return vegetables to skillet. Add remaining broth and noodles. Cook, tossing, 1 to 2 minutes, until sauce thickens slightly. Serve at once.

PER SERVING   Calories 232   Total Fat 4 g   Saturated Fat 1 g
Cholesterol 35 mg   Percentage calories from fat 14%

Savory Italian Pie

Makes 4 servings

4 sheets thawed frozen phyllo dough

1 cup part-skim ricotta cheese

½ cup egg substitute

¼ cup grated reduced-fat Parmesan cheese

½ teaspoon basil

½ teaspoon oregano

¼ teaspoon freshly ground black pepper

1 cup mushroom-flavored reduced-calorie spaghetti sauce

3 ounces thinly sliced fat-free mozzarella cheese

8 plum tomatoes, thinly sliced

½ cup thinly sliced mushrooms

1. Preheat oven to 425 degrees F. Place one sheet of phyllo dough into bottom of an 11 by 7-inch baking dish. Coat phyllo lightly with nonstick cooking spray. Top with another sheet of phyllo and spray lightly. Repeat with 2 remaining sheets to make 4 layers. Fold edges of phyllo over to make a crust that lines dish. Bake 5 minutes, or until phyllo begins to brown.

2. Meanwhile, in a medium bowl, combine ricotta cheese, egg substitute, Parmesan cheese, basil, oregano, and pepper. Blend well.

3. Remove baking pan from oven. Spoon half of ricotta mixture into phyllo crust, spreading evenly. Top with ½ cup spaghetti sauce. Sprinkle half of mozzarella over sauce and cover with half of tomato slices. Scatter ¼ cup mushroom slices over tomatoes. Repeat with remaining ingredients to make 1 more layer.

4. Bake 15 to 20 minutes, until crust is golden.

PER SERVNG   Calories 167   Total Fat 5 g   Saturated Fat 3 g
Cholesterol 17 mg   Percent calories from fat 25%

Pepperoni Pie

Makes 6 servings

This dish incorporates all the flavors of your favorite pizza. Serve with a big green salad.

½ cup thinly sliced turkey pepperoni

1 medium tomato, coarsely chopped

1 medium green bell pepper, coarsely chopped

½ teaspoon dried basil

½ teaspoon dried oregano

1 cup reduced-fat buttermilk baking mix

1 cup skim milk

½ cup egg substitute

1 tablespoon grated Parmesan cheese

½ cup nonfat shredded mozzarella cheese

½ cup reduced-calorie spaghetti sauce

1. Preheat oven to 425 degrees F. Coat a 9-inch pie plate with nonstick cooking spray. Add pepperoni, tomatoes, pepper, basil, and oregano to pie plate and toss to mix.

2. In a medium bowl, combine baking mix, milk, egg substitute, and Parmesan cheese. Beat until blended. Pour over pepperoni mixture. Bake 12 minutes. Sprinkle mozzarella cheese over top and bake 4 to 5 minutes longer, until cheese melts and crust is golden.

3. Meanwhile, heat spaghetti sauce in a microwave or over stovetop. Serve pie in wedges, topped with spaghetti sauce.

PER SERVING   Calories 144   Total Fat 3 g   Saturated Fat 1 g
Cholesterol 8 mg   Percentage calories from fat 17%

Prosciutto and Potato Frittata

Makes 4 servings

1 cup chopped scallions

2 garlic cloves, minced

1 ½ cups egg substitute

4 ounces reduced-fat Jarlsberg cheese, shredded

½ teaspoon dried thyme

¼ teaspoon salt

¼ teaspoon freshly ground black pepper

¾ pound red potatoes, cooked and thinly sliced

1 ounce prosciutto or baked ham, finely chopped

1 tablespoon grated provolone cheese

¼ teaspoon paprika

1. Preheat broiler. Coat a large ovenproof skillet with nonstick cooking spray; heat skillet over medium heat. Add scallions and garlic; cook, stirring often, 2 to 3 minutes, until scallions are wilted and garlic is soft.

2. In a medium bowl, whisk together egg substitute, Jarlsberg cheese, thyme, salt, and pepper. Pour into skillet, stirring gently to mix in scallions and garlic. Reduce heat to low. Arrange potato slices over eggs. Scatter prosciutto on top. Cover skillet and cook until eggs are almost set, 6 to 8 minutes.

3. Sprinkle provolone cheese and paprika over frittata. Transfer skillet to broiler and broil about 6 inches from heat 2 to 3 minutes, until eggs are set, edges are golden, and provolone is melted. Serve warm, at room temperature, or even slightly chilled.

PER SERVING   Calories 229   Total Fat 6 g   Saturated Fat 3 g
Cholesterol 22 mg   Percentage calories from fat 24%

Curried Lamb with Spinach

Makes 4 servings

A traditional curry is a mixture of several spices blended to make a strong, flavorful dish. It is perfect for low-fat cooking because flavor is achieved without adding extra fat and calories.

1 teaspoon olive oil
1 medium onion, chopped
10 ounces lean lamb cubes
1 (14½-ounce) can diced tomatoes
1½ teaspoons turmeric
1½ teaspoons ground cumin
1½ teaspoons ground coriander
½ teaspoon salt
¼ teaspoon cinnamon
Pinch cloves
1 (10-ounce) package frozen chopped spinach, thawed and
   squeezed dry
¾ cup reduced-sodium beef broth
2 tablespoons red wine vinegar
4 cups steamed rice

1. In a large nonstick skillet, heat oil over medium-high heat. Add onion and cook, stirring often, until softened, about 3 minutes. Add lamb cubes and cook, tossing, until browned, 3 to 5 minutes longer.

2. Stir in tomatoes, turmeric, cumin, coriander, salt, cinnamon, and cloves; bring to a boil. Reduce heat to low. Stir in spinach, broth, and vinegar. Cover and simmer 10 to 12 minutes, until lamb is tender and liquid has thickened slightly.

3. To serve, spread 1 cup rice on each dinner plate. Top with equal amounts of lamb curry.

PER SERVING   Calories 433   Total Fat 6 g   Saturated Fat 2 g
Cholesterol 46 mg   Percentage calories from fat 13%

Baked Sole with Fennel, Carrots, and Rice

Makes 4 servings

2 cups instant rice

4 (5- to 6-ounce) sole or flounder fillets

¼ teaspoon paprika

¼ teaspoon salt

¼ teaspoon freshly ground black pepper

2 tablespoons fresh lemon juice

1 cup finely chopped fresh fennel or celery

1 cup finely chopped carrots

1 teaspoon dried thyme

2 tablespoons chopped flat-leaf parsley

½ cup boiling chicken broth

1. Preheat oven to 350 degrees F. In a small saucepan, bring 2 cups water to a boil. Stir in rice, cover, and remove from heat. Let stand, covered, 5 minutes.

2. Coat an 11 by 7-inch baking pan with nonstick cooking spray. Spread rice evenly into bottom of pan. Place fish fillets on top of rice. Season sole with paprika, salt, and pepper. Sprinkle with lemon juice. Scatter fennel and carrots over fish and sprinkle thyme and parsley on top. Pour broth over all.

3. Cover baking pan with foil. Bake 10 to 12 minutes, until fish turns opaque and flakes when prodded gently with a fork.

PER SERVING   Calories 341   Total Fat 2 g   Saturated Fat 1 g
Cholesterol 68 mg   Percentage calories from fat 7%

Supper Salad

Makes 4 servings

Because there is no cooking involved, this meal-in-a-bowl salad is perfect for a hot summer night. Orange juice replaces much of the oil in the dressing.

¼ cup red wine vinegar

2 tablespoons orange juice

1 tablespoon extra-virgin olive oil

1 tablespoon finely chopped sweet pickle

1 garlic clove, minced

½ teaspoon dried basil

6 cups stale whole grain bread cubes

2 cups coarsely chopped romaine lettuce

2 cups coarsely chopped red leaf lettuce

1 (6¼-ounce) can water-packed tuna, drained and flaked

4 ounces nonfat mozzarella cheese, cut into ½-inch dice

1 red bell pepper, cut into thin strips

1 cup thawed frozen peas

1 tablespoon grated Parmesan cheese

1. In a large salad bowl, whisk together vinegar, orange juice, olive oil, pickle, garlic, and basil.

2. Add remaining ingredients except Parmesan cheese. Toss to mix well and coat with dressing. Let stand 5 minutes to soften bread cubes slightly.

3. Just before serving, sprinkle with Parmesan and toss to mix.

PER SERVING   Calories 279   Total Fat 6 g   Saturated Fat 1 g
Cholesterol 23 mg   Percentage calories from fat 19%

Ham and Egg Fried Rice

Makes 4 servings

Leftover rice and cooked meats can turn your kitchen into a Chinese take-out in a flash. I've used ham here, but you can substitute whatever meat or fish you have on hand. For vegetarian eaters, try beans or tofu instead of meat. If you don't have any leftover rice, put up a pot of instant before beginning.

2 tablespoons slivered almonds

1 teaspoon peanut oil

1 cup chopped scallions

½ cup shredded carrots

1 tablespoon grated fresh ginger

1 cup egg substitute

2 tablespoons skim milk

¼ teaspoon salt

4 ounces sliced reduced-fat ham, cut into ½-inch-wide strips

2 cups cooked brown rice

1 tablespoon teriyaki sauce

1. Heat a nonstick wok or large skillet over medium heat. Add almonds and cook, stirring constantly, 1 to 2 minutes, until golden brown. Immediately remove from wok and set aside.

2. In same wok or skillet, heat oil over medium-high heat. Add scallions, carrots, and ginger. Cook, stirring often, 3 to 4 minutes, until carrots are crisp-tender.

3. In a medium bowl, beat together egg substitute, milk, and salt, until blended. Add to skillet and cook, stirring often, 3 to 4 minutes, until eggs begin to set and are partially cooked. Add ham; cook 1 to 2 minutes longer, until eggs are set.

4. Add rice and teriyaki sauce. Cook, stirring often, 4 to 5 minutes, until rice is browned and slightly crisp. Sprinkle with almonds and serve.

PER SERVING   Calories 236   Total Fat 6 g   Saturated Fat 1 g
Cholesterol 15 mg   Percentage calories from fat 22%

Cheese Enchilada Casserole

Makes 4 servings

Mexican food is still a number-one favorite in many families. This dish brings a restaurant favorite home by combining ideas from several classics.

3 large (10-ounce) flour tortillas
1½ cups medium salsa
1 (16-ounce) can black beans, rinsed and drained
1 medium tomato, chopped
1 cup corn kernels, canned or thawed frozen
1 small onion, chopped
1 cup shredded reduced-fat Cheddar cheese

1. Preheat oven to 400 degrees F. Coat a 2-quart ovenproof casserole with nonstick cooking spray.

2. Place 1 tortilla in bottom of casserole. Spread ½ cup salsa over tortilla. Sprinkle with half of the beans, tomatoes, corn, onion, and ⅓ cup cheese. Add another tortilla; repeat toppings to make another layer. Cover with third tortilla. Spread remaining ½ cup salsa over last tortilla and sprinkle remaining ⅓ cup cheese over top.

3. Bake 15 to 20 minutes, until heated through. Serve, cut in wedges.

PER SERVING   Calories 464   Total Fat 11 g   Saturated Fat 4 g
Cholesterol 20 mg   Percentage calories from fat 22%

Corn Chili with Black Beans

Makes 4 servings

To *dress up chili, I like to pass a variety of accompaniments: baked tortilla chips, nonfat sour cream, pickled jalapeños, red onion, and tomato.*

1 teaspoon olive oil
1 cup chopped scallions
1 green bell pepper, chopped
1 red bell pepper, chopped
1 (16-ounce) can corn kernels, drained
1 (14-ounce) can stewed tomatoes
1 cup canned black beans, rinsed and drained
¼ pound reduced-fat smoked ham, coarsely chopped
2 tablespoons chopped canned green chiles
2 teaspoons red wine vinegar
1 teaspoon chili powder
½ cup shredded reduced-fat Monterey Jack cheese

1. In a large saucepan, heat oil over medium-high heat. Add scallions and bell peppers; cook, stirring constantly, 4 to 5 minutes, until peppers are softened.

2. Stir in all remaining ingredients except cheese. Bring to a boil; reduce heat to medium-low. Simmer 10 minutes.

3. To serve, ladle into bowls. Sprinkle 2 tablespoons shredded cheese on top of each portion.

PER SERVING   Calories 278   Total Fat 6 g   Saturated Fat 3 g
Cholesterol 23 mg   Percentage calories from fat 18%

Peppers Stuffed with Orzo and Feta Cheese

Makes 4 servings

1 cup orzo

4 medium green bell peppers

3 cups reduced-calorie spaghetti sauce

2 cups thawed frozen mixed vegetables

½ cup crumbled herb-flavored feta cheese

¼ cup seasoned dry bread crumbs

1 teaspoon paprika

1. Preheat oven to 400 degrees F. In a medium saucepan of boiling salted water, cook orzo 6 to 8 minutes, until tender but still firm; drain.

2. Meanwhile, cut tops off peppers. Carefully scoop out seeds and ribs. Place peppers, cut side up, on a microwave-safe plate and microwave on high 2 minutes, rotating them halfway through, to soften slightly.

3. Spoon ¼ cup orzo into each pepper. Top with ¼ cup spaghetti sauce, one-fourth of vegetables, and 1 tablespoon feta cheese. Repeat to make one more layer. Sprinkle 1 tablespoon bread crumbs and ¼ teaspoon paprika over top of each pepper.

4. Pour remaining sauce into bottom of an 8-inch-square baking pan. Arrange stuffed peppers in pan. Bake 10 to 15 minutes, until heated through. Serve peppers with sauce from pan.

PER SERVING   Calories 416   Total Fat 6 g   Saturated Fat 3 g
Cholesterol 12 mg   Percentage calories from fat 13%

Vegetable Stir-Fry with Couscous and Mushrooms

Makes 4 servings

*S*tir-fries make great one-pot dinners. With the addition of couscous, this dish becomes complete with no additional pots or long cooking times for the grain.

2 teaspoons Asian sesame oil

6 ounces firm tofu, well drained and cut into ¾-inch cubes

1 medium onion, chopped

1 medium red bell pepper, cut into strips

1 medium green bell pepper, cut into strips

10 ounces mushrooms, thinly sliced

¼ pound snow peas

1 cup reduced-sodium chicken broth

½ cup orange juice

1 cup quick-cooking couscous

1 cup shredded napa (Chinese) cabbage

1. In a nonstick wok or large skillet, heat 1 teaspoon sesame oil over medium-high heat. Add tofu and cook, stirring often, 3 to 4 minutes, until golden.

2. Heat remaining 1 teaspoon oil in wok. Add onion, peppers, and mushrooms. Stir-fry over high heat 3 to 4 minutes, until vegetables are crisp-tender. Add snow peas and stir-fry 1 minute longer.

3. Pour broth and juice into skillet and bring to a boil. Stir in couscous and cabbage. Remove from heat; cover and let stand 5 minutes. Fluff couscous with a fork before serving.

PER SERVING Calories 341 Total Fat 7 g Saturated Fat 1 g
Cholesterol 0 mg Percentage calories from fat 18%

Quick and Savory
Vegetables and
Sides

Foods that accompany a main course can be truly exciting and should be just as important both in taste and nutrition as the "main event." In fact, for many people, the sides are the best part of the meal. As we've learned the nutritional value of vegetables in any well-balanced, low-fat diet, many of us have come to a new appreciation of their beauty, both in terms of eye appeal as well as taste.

Here you'll find many familiar vegetable dishes, but all with a new twist. Spicy Corn Cakes and Buttermilk Mashed Potatoes provide tasty, low-fat versions of American classics. Orange-Pineapple Beets and Blue Cheese Cauliflower Puree with Chives treat common vegetables in uncommon ways. And the addition of international ingredients adds interest and appeal in the East-West blends you'll find in Two-Squash Stir-Fry with Ginger and Cilantro and Curried Mixed Vegetables.

Most of these recipes are versatile enough to go with almost any simple lean meat, chicken, or fish of your choice. And whichever you choose, rest assured, it will be low in fat and ready in nothing flat.

Artichoke and Oat Gratin

Makes 4 servings

*T*hough a bit unexpected in a vegetable dish, oats impart a great nutty taste and extra note of texture to this lovely casserole.

10 dry-pack sun-dried tomato halves

1 cup boiling water

½ cup finely chopped scallions

½ cup quick-cooking oats

2 tablespoons seasoned dry bread crumbs

1 (10-ounce) box thawed frozen artichoke hearts

1 (7-ounce) jar roasted red peppers, drained and coarsely chopped

2 tablespoons fat-free mayonnaise

½ teaspoon dried basil

¼ teaspoon freshly ground black pepper

1 tablespoon grated Parmesan cheese

1. Place dried tomatoes in a small bowl. Cover with boiling water. Let stand 5 to 10 minutes, until softened. Drain, reserving ¼ cup soaking liquid.

2. Meanwhile, preheat oven to 375 degrees F. Coat a large oven-proof skillet with nonstick cooking spray; heat skillet over medium-high heat. Add scallions and cook, stirring often, 2 minutes, or until wilted. Stir in oats and bread crumbs; cook 2 to 3 minutes longer, until oats are golden brown.

3. Add drained tomatoes to skillet along with ¼ cup reserved liquid, artichokes, roasted peppers, mayonnaise, basil, and black pepper. Cook, stirring, 2 to 3 minutes longer, until liquid evaporates.

4. Sprinkle Parmesan cheese over vegetables. Transfer skillet to the oven. Bake 8 to 10 minutes, until cheese is melted and golden.

PER SERVING   Calories 135   Total Fat 2 g   Saturated Fat 1 g
Cholesterol 1 mg   Percentage calories from fat 12%

Orange-Pineapple Beets

Makes 4 servings

1 pound small fresh beets, peeled and sliced
1¼ cups reduced-sodium chicken broth
1 tablespoon reduced-calorie margarine
1 teaspoon whole cloves
¼ cup orange-pineapple juice
1½ teaspoons grated orange zest
1 tablespoon chopped fresh tarragon or 1 teaspoon dried
2 teaspoons brown sugar

1. In a large nonstick skillet, combine beets, broth, margarine, and cloves. Bring broth to a boil; reduce heat to medium-low, cover, and cook 10 minutes.

2. Uncover and cook 5 minutes longer, until beets are just tender and almost all liquid has evaporated.

3. Stir in juice, orange zest, tarragon, and brown sugar. Boil 5 minutes, spooning liquid over beets, until juice thickens to a glaze.

PER SERVING   Calories 76   Total Fat 2 g   Saturated Fat <1 g
Cholesterol 0 mg   Percentage calories from fat 19%

Broccoli with Creamy Mustard Sauce

Makes 4 servings

This creamy mustard sauce is lightened up by using skim milk and low-fat cheese. The result is a wonderful sauce that can be used not just for vegetables, but also over grilled poultry and seafood.

½ pound broccoli florets (about 6 cups)
1 tablespoon plus 1 teaspoon reduced-calorie margarine
2 tablespoons flour
½ cup skim milk
½ cup chicken broth
¾ cup shredded low-fat Cheddar cheese (about 3 ounces)
1½ tablespoons Dijon mustard
1 tablespoon chopped fresh parsley
¼ teaspoon paprika
Pinch ground white pepper

1. Place broccoli florets in a steamer basket over gently simmering water. Cover and steam broccoli 5 to 10 minutes, until tender.

2. Meanwhile, in a small saucepan, melt margarine over medium heat. Stir in flour; cook, stirring constantly, 1 minute. Stir in milk and broth; cook, stirring constantly, 2 to 3 minutes, until sauce boils and thickens slightly.

3. Gradually stir in cheese, mustard, parsley, paprika, and pepper until cheese melts. Spoon sauce over steamed broccoli and serve.

PER SERVING   Calories 166   Total Fat 6 g   Saturated Fat 3 g
Cholesterol 16 mg   Percentage calories from fat 30%

Parsleyed Broccoli Rabe and Chickpeas

Makes 4 servings

Broccoli rabe has a lovely mild bite that perks up even the simplest of vegetable dishes. You can substitute ordinary broccoli here if you prefer, but the dish will not be quite as interesting.

2 teaspoons olive oil

2 cinnamon sticks

1 bunch broccoli rabe, cut into 1-inch pieces

1 cup chopped scallions

2 garlic cloves, minced

1 (15-ounce) can chickpeas, rinsed and drained

3 tablespoons chopped fresh parsley

1 tablespoon fresh lemon juice

¼ teaspoon salt

¼ teaspoon freshly ground black pepper

1. In a large nonstick skillet, heat oil over medium-high heat. Add cinnamon sticks and cook, stirring sticks often, 1 minute. Add broccoli rabe, scallions, and garlic. Cook, stirring often, 4 to 5 minutes, until broccoli rabe is just tender.

2. Add chickpeas and cook 2 minutes, until heated through. Stir in parsley, lemon juice, salt, and pepper; cook 1 minute longer to blend flavors.

PER SERVING   Calories 125   Total Fat 4 g   Saturated Fat <1 g
Cholesterol 0 mg   Percentage calories from fat 28%

Crispy Cabbage Slaw

Makes 4 servings

½ cup cider vinegar

¼ cup orange juice

¼ cup sugar

1 teaspoon Dijon mustard

¼ teaspoon salt

2 teaspoons olive oil

1 ½ teaspoons mustard seeds

½ teaspoon celery seeds

1 ½ cups shredded red cabbage

1 ½ cups shredded green cabbage

1 cup julienned snow peas (about 3 ounces)

1 medium red bell pepper, cut into thin strips

1. In a small saucepan, combine vinegar, orange juice, sugar, mustard, salt, and ¼ cup water. Bring to a boil; reduce heat to medium. Boil 2 to 3 minutes, until liquid is reduced to about ¼ cup. Remove from heat and cover to keep warm.

2. In a large nonstick skillet, heat oil over medium-high heat. Add mustard seeds and celery seeds. Cook 1 minute, or until seeds begin to pop. Add red and green cabbage, snow peas, and bell pepper. Cook, stirring often, 4 to 5 minutes, until vegetables are crisp-tender.

3. Pour vinegar mixture over vegetables and cook 1 minute longer. Serve warm or at room temperature. If slaw stands or is refrigerated, toss before serving.

PER SERVING   Calories 122   Total Fat 3 g   Saturated Fat <1 g
Cholesterol 0 mg   Percentage calories from fat 20%

Spicy Corn Cakes

Makes 4 servings, approximately 8 corn cakes

½ cup nonfat plain yogurt

¼ cup chopped roasted red peppers

1 tablespoon minced scallions

1 tablespoon chopped fresh cilantro

1 teaspoon lime juice

1½ cups thawed frozen corn kernels

½ cup egg substitute

1½ tablespoons flour

1 teaspoon sugar

½ teaspoon chili powder

¼ teaspoon ground cumin

¼ teaspoon salt

2 teaspoons olive oil

1. In a small bowl, combine yogurt, red peppers, scallions, cilantro, and lime juice. Stir to blend well.

2. Place corn kernels in a food processor. Process until coarsely chopped. Add egg substitute, flour, sugar, chili powder, cumin, and salt. Process until well blended but not smooth.

3. In a large nonstick skillet, heat oil over medium heat. Add batter by scant ¼ cupfuls and cook about 3 minutes, or until bubbles start to form on top. Flip cakes over and cook 3 to 4 minutes longer, until golden brown on both sides. Serve corn cakes with yogurt topping.

PER SERVING   Calories 125   Total Fat 3 g   Saturated Fat <1 g
Cholesterol 1 mg   Percentage calories from fat 20%

Cauliflower with Celery and Orange

Makes 4 servings

1 medium head cauliflower (about 2 pounds), separated into
    florets
2 large carrots, thinly sliced
1 tablespoon reduced-calorie margarine
1 red onion, thinly sliced and separated into rings
2 garlic cloves, minced
½ cup orange juice
¼ cup golden raisins
¼ teaspoon ground ginger
Pinch cayenne
Salt

1. Place cauliflower and carrots in a steamer basket over simmering water. Cover and steam 6 to 8 minutes, until tender.

2. In a large nonstick skillet, melt margarine over medium-high heat. Add red onion and garlic and cook, stirring often, 3 to 4 minutes, until onion is tender. Stir in orange juice, raisins, ginger, and cayenne. Bring to a boil; reduce heat to low.

3. Add cauliflower and carrots to skillet. Cover and cook 2 minutes, spooning sauce over vegetables, to blend flavors. Season with salt to taste before serving.

PER SERVING   Calories 116   Total Fat 2 g   Saturated Fat <1 g
Cholesterol 0 mg   Percentage calories from fat 12%

Blue Cheese Cauliflower Puree with Chives

Makes 4 servings

This robust vegetable dish is great served with a simple roasted chicken or grilled meats. Because blue cheese is potent, a little goes a long way.

1 pound cauliflower florets
½ cup skim milk
2 tablespoons chopped chives
1 garlic clove, crushed through a press
1 teaspoon dried oregano
¼ teaspoon salt
¼ teaspoon freshly ground black pepper
1 ounce crumbled blue cheese (about ¼ cup)
2 teaspoons herbed white wine vinegar or cider vinegar

1. In a large pot of boiling salted water, cook cauliflower 5 to 7 minutes, until soft. Drain into a colander.

2. In a small saucepan, combine milk, chives, garlic, oregano, salt, and pepper. Cook over medium heat 1 to 2 minutes, until hot but not boiling.

3. Transfer cauliflower to food processor. Add hot milk mixture, blue cheese, and vinegar. Puree until smooth. Serve hot.

PER SERVING   Calories 66   Total Fat 2 g   Saturated Fat 1 g
Cholesterol 6 mg   Percentage calories from fat 29%

Green Beans with Sunflower Seeds

Makes 6 servings

*S*unflower seeds may sound like an unusual garnish, but they provide a nice change of pace from sesame seeds and contribute extra protein as well as vitamins and minerals. Sugar snap peas also work well with this treatment, though their cooking time will be slightly shorter.

1 ½ teaspoons olive oil

1 tablespoon sunflower seeds

¼ cup chopped red onion

1 ½ pounds green beans, trimmed

2 garlic cloves, crushed through a press

¼ cup chicken broth or water

1 tablespoon teriyaki sauce

2 teaspoons fresh lemon juice

1 teaspoon grated lemon zest

1. In a large nonstick skillet, heat ½ teaspoon oil over medium heat. Add sunflower seeds; cook, stirring constantly, 1 to 2 minutes, until lightly golden brown. Remove seeds from skillet and set aside.

2. Add remaining 1 teaspoon oil and red onion to skillet. Cook over medium-high heat, stirring often, 2 to 3 minutes, until softened. Add green beans and garlic; toss to mix and coat with oil. Cook, stirring often, 2 minutes.

3. Add chicken broth, teriyaki sauce, lemon juice, and lemon zest. Cover skillet and cook 4 to 5 minutes longer, until beans are just tender. Transfer to a bowl, sprinkle sunflower seeds on top, and serve.

PER SERVING   Calories 57   Total Fat 2 g   Saturated Fat 0 g
Cholesterol 0 mg   Percentage calories from fat 28%

Stir-Fried Greens with Garlic and Walnuts

Makes 4 servings

To save time, look for packaged prewashed spinach that's all ready to use. Watercress adds a pleasing bite to the blander spinach.

1½ tablespoons coarsely chopped walnuts
1 teaspoon vegetable oil
1 large red onion, thinly sliced and separated into rings
4 garlic cloves, thinly sliced
1 pound recipe-ready spinach leaves
1 large or 2 small bunches watercress, tough stems removed
     (about ½ pound)
1 cup cherry tomatoes, sliced in half
2 tablespoons dry white wine or chicken broth
¼ teaspoon salt
¼ teaspoon freshly ground black pepper

1. Heat a large nonstick skillet over medium heat. Add walnuts and cook, stirring often, 1 to 2 minutes, until lightly toasted. Remove to a small dish.

2. Add oil, red onion, and garlic to skillet. Cook over medium-high heat, stirring often, 3 to 4 minutes, until onions are tender.

3. Stir in spinach and watercress, adding greens gradually if necessary so they fit in pan. Add tomatoes, wine, salt, and pepper. Cook, stirring often, 2 to 3 minutes, until greens are wilted but still bright green. Sprinkle with toasted walnuts and serve.

PER SERVING   Calories 97   Total Fat 4 g   Saturated Fat <1 g
Cholesterol 0 mg   Percentage calories from fat 29%

Sautéed Wild Mushrooms and Asparagus

Makes 4 servings

1 tablespoon reduced-calorie margarine

¼ cup minced onion

1 tablespoon grated fresh ginger

1 teaspoon grated lemon zest

1 pound thin asparagus, ends trimmed

6 ounces shiitake, stemmed, or cremini mushrooms

¼ cup chicken broth

1 teaspoon Worcestershire sauce

1. In a large nonstick skillet, melt margarine over medium-high heat. Add onion and cook, stirring often, 2 to 3 minutes, until softened.

2. Stir in ginger and lemon zest; cook 1 minute. Add asparagus and mushrooms and cook, tossing, 2 to 3 minutes, until mushrooms start to give up their juices.

3. Add chicken broth and Worcestershire sauce. Cover skillet and cook 1 to 2 minutes longer, until asparagus is just tender. Serve hot.

PER SERVING   Calories 56   Total Fat 2 g   Saturated Fat <1 g
Cholesterol 0 mg   Percentage calories from fat 25%

Buttermilk Mashed Potatoes

Makes 4 servings

Buttermilk is now commonly available in low-fat form. It adds a wonderful nuttiness and semblance of richness without excessive calories or fat. Garlic and horseradish give these potatoes an extra flavor boost.

2 pounds baking potatoes, peeled and cut into 1-inch chunks
4 whole garlic cloves
½ cup low-fat buttermilk
¼ cup nonfat sour cream
1 tablespoon prepared white horseradish
1 tablespoon chopped fresh parsley
½ teaspoon salt
¼ teaspoon freshly ground black pepper

1. In a large saucepan of boiling salted water, cook potatoes and garlic 15 to 18 minutes, until potatoes are tender. Drain, reserving 2 tablespoons cooking water.

2. Place potatoes, garlic, and reserved liquid in a large bowl. Beat with an electric mixer to mash coarsely.

3. Add buttermilk, sour cream, horseradish, parsley, salt, and pepper. Beat until mashed potatoes are smooth, but do not overmix or they may become sticky.

PER SERVING   Calories 197   Total Fat 1 g   Saturated Fat <1 g
Cholesterol 2 mg   Percentage calories from fat 4%

Spinach and Apple Pilaf

Makes 4 servings

1 ounce sliced almonds (about 2 tablespoons)

1 teaspoon olive oil

¼ cup chopped shallots

1 small Granny Smith apple, cored, peeled, and chopped

1 tablespoon fresh lemon juice

1 (10-ounce) box frozen chopped spinach, thawed and
squeezed dry

2 tablespoons chopped fresh dill or 1½ teaspoons dried

2 tablespoons chopped fresh parsley

¼ teaspoon salt

¼ teaspoon freshly ground black pepper

1 cup reduced-sodium chicken broth

½ cup unsweetened apple juice

1 cup quick-cooking couscous

1. In a large dry skillet, toast almonds over medium heat, stirring often, until they are golden and just beginning to brown, 2 to 3 minutes. Immediately remove nuts and set aside.

2. Add oil and shallots to skillet and cook, stirring often, 2 minutes, or until softened. Add apples and lemon juice; toss to mix. Cook 3 to 4 minutes, until apples are tender. Stir in spinach, dill, parsley, salt, and pepper.

3. Add broth and apple juice to saucepan. Raise heat and bring to a boil. Stir in couscous and reserved almonds. Cover and remove saucepan from heat. Let stand 5 minutes. Fluff pilaf with fork and serve.

PER SERVING   Calories 285   Total Fat 5 g   Saturated Fat 1 g
Cholesterol 0 mg   Percentage calories from fat 17%

Sweetly Spiced Acorn Squash

Makes 4 servings

2 medium acorn squash (about 1 pound each)

7 pitted prunes, halved

½ cup apple juice

2 tablespoons reduced-calorie margarine, melted

2 tablespoons reduced-calorie pancake syrup

1 tablespoon firmly packed brown sugar

½ teaspoon cinnamon

⅛ teaspoon nutmeg

Pinch ground cloves

1. Prick each squash in several places with tip of a knife. Microwave on high, turning once or twice, 5 minutes, or until slightly softened. Cut squash into 1-inch rings.

2. Preheat oven to 425 degrees F. Coat a large shallow baking dish with nonstick cooking spray. Place squash rings in dish. Scatter prunes over squash.

3. In a small bowl, combine apple juice, margarine, pancake syrup, brown sugar, cinnamon, nutmeg, and cloves. Stir to mix well. Pour over squash.

4. Bake 15 to 20 minutes, basting with sauce in dish several times, until squash is tender.

PER SERVING   Calories 172   Total Fat 3 g   Saturated Fat 1 g
Cholesterol 0 mg   Percentage calories from fat 16%

Two-Squash Stir-Fry with Ginger and Cilantro

Makes 4 servings

Sesame oil, soy sauce, and scallions ensure that this colorful dish is packed with good taste. While it is suggested here as a side dish, you may find you like it so much you want to serve it over brown rice as a vegetarian main course.

¼ teaspoon cayenne

1¼ teaspoons Asian sesame oil

2 tablespoons soy sauce

1 tablespoon seasoned rice wine vinegar

1 tablespoon honey

1 teaspoon olive oil

1 tablespoon grated fresh ginger

3 medium zucchini, thinly sliced

2 medium yellow squash, thinly sliced

½ cup chopped scallions

3 tablespoons chicken broth or water

2 tablespoons chopped fresh cilantro

1. In a small saucepan, cook cayenne in sesame oil over medium heat 1 minute. Add soy sauce, vinegar, and honey; cook, stirring, 30 seconds. Remove from heat and set sauce aside.

2. In a nonstick wok or large skillet, heat olive oil over medium-high heat. Add ginger and cook, stirring constantly, 30 seconds. Add zucchini, squash, and scallions. Stir-fry 3 minutes. Add broth and cook 2 minutes longer, or until vegetables are just tender.

3. Pour sauce over squash. Add cilantro and cook, stirring, 1 minute longer. Serve at once.

PER SERVING   Calories 79   Total Fat 3 g   Saturated Fat <1 g
Cholesterol 0 mg   Percentage calories from fat 30%

Creamy Basil-Topped Tomatoes

Makes 4 servings

Whether you serve these pretty red tomatoes with their green topping as a side dish or garnish, they are a tasty addition to any plate.

2 large ripe tomatoes

¼ cup nonfat plain yogurt

¼ cup nonfat sour cream

2 teaspoons flour

2 tablespoons chopped fresh basil

2 teaspoons sweet pickle relish

¼ teaspoon salt

¼ teaspoon freshly ground black pepper

3 tablespoons grated provolone cheese

½ teaspoon paprika

1. Preheat oven to 425 degrees F. Coat an 8-inch-square baking pan with nonstick cooking spray. Core tomatoes with as shallow a cut as possible. Cut tomatoes in half horizontally and squeeze gently to remove seeds. Place tomatoes upside down on paper towels to drain.

2. In a small bowl, combine yogurt, sour cream, flour, basil, pickle relish, salt, and pepper. Mix to blend well. Place tomatoes, cut sides up, in baking pan. Spoon equal amounts of yogurt mixture on tops of tomatoes.

3. Sprinkle provolone cheese evenly over tomatoes and dust with paprika. Bake tomatoes 10 to 15 minutes, until tops are golden brown. Serve hot.

PER SERVING   Calories 64   Total Fat 2 g   Saturated Fat 1 g
Cholesterol 4 mg   Percentage calories from fat 27%

Zesty Vegetables Vinaigrette

Makes 4 servings

2 tablespoons balsamic vinegar

2 tablespoons finely chopped roasted red peppers (jarred are fine)

1 tablespoon finely chopped pitted ripe or kalamata olives

1 tablespoon finely chopped capers

1 tablespoon finely chopped fresh parsley

½ teaspoon salt

2 teaspoons olive oil

1 medium eggplant (about 1¼ pounds), cut into 1-inch cubes

1 large zucchini, coarsely chopped

1 large green bell pepper, cut into thin strips

1 medium tomato, seeded and coarsely chopped

1. In a small bowl, combine vinegar, roasted peppers, olives, capers, parsley, and salt. Whisk in oil until well blended. Set vinaigrette aside.

2. Coat a large nonstick skillet with nonstick cooking spray; heat skillet over medium-high heat. Add eggplant and cook, stirring often, 2 minutes. Add zucchini and bell pepper and cook, stirring often, 5 to 7 minutes, until vegetables are tender. Stir in tomato and cook 1 minute longer to heat through.

3. To serve, transfer vegetables to a large serving bowl. Pour on vinaigrette and toss to mix well. Serve hot, at room temperature, or slightly chilled.

PER SERVING   Calories 83   Total Fat 3 g   Saturated Fat <1 g
Cholesterol 0 mg   Percentage calories from fat 30%

Curried Mixed Vegetables

Makes 4 servings

¼ cup vegetable broth

2 tablespoons soy sauce

1 tablespoon hoisin sauce

½ teaspoon sugar

¼ teaspoon freshly ground black pepper

1 tablespoon peanut oil

1 ½ tablespoons minced fresh ginger

1 tablespoon curry powder

4 cups finely shredded savoy cabbage

2 cups shredded carrots

1 medium onion, thinly sliced

1 medium red bell pepper, cut into thin strips

1 green bell pepper, cut into thin strips

1 ½ tablespoons Chinese rice wine or dry white wine

1 cup fresh bean sprouts

½ cup canned water chestnut slices

1. In a small bowl, combine broth, soy sauce, hoisin sauce, sugar, and pepper. Set sauce aside.

2. In a nonstick wok or large skillet, heat oil until very hot over high heat. Add ginger and curry; cook 30 seconds. Add cabbage, carrots, onion, bell peppers, and wine. Stir-fry 4 to 5 minutes, until vegetables are crisp-tender.

3. Add bean sprouts, water chestnuts, and reserved sauce. Stir-fry 1 to 2 minutes longer, until liquid is reduced by half.

PER SERVING   Calories 148   Total Fat 4 g   Saturated Fat 1 g
Cholesterol 0 mg   Percentage calories from fat 23%

Almost Instant
Low-Fat Desserts

Without a doubt, dessert is the showstopper, finale, and oftentimes the downfall of a well-balanced and carefully considered meal. I was determined in this book to provide an assortment of sweet indulgences that could be enjoyed along with any sensible meal. So here they are: old favorites reworked to meet today's nutritional demands and new delectable after-dinner sweets—all coming in at 30 percent or less calories from fat.

Certain well-conceived products, such as fruit juice concentrates, unsweetened cocoa powder, nonfat plain and flavored yogurts, egg substitute, reduced-calorie margarine, and varied spices, as well as good nonstick cookware, make these culinary reworks possible. They should be a staple in your dessert pantry. Fresh fruits and berries, of course, also play a large part in this chapter, since they are naturally practically fat-free.

Whether you're looking for a sweet snack, a pretty dessert, or just a light refreshment after the meal, you're sure to find a favorite here. Recipes range from Old-Fashioned Oatmeal Cookies, Cocoa Crisps, and Raisin Cake to Quick Blueberry-Peach Cobblers, Apple-Apricot Tartlets, and even Peanut Fudge Truffles.

A nice side benefit of low-fat desserts is that they also tend to be low in calories. With the exception of a couple of recipes, all the sweets in this chapter contain well below 200 calories per serving, a fact that makes indulgence doubly pleasurable.

Apple-Apricot Tartlets

Makes 4 servings

Refrigerated biscuit dough forms the crust for these quick and simple tarts. Look in the refrigerated section of your supermarket for low-fat varieties of the biscuits.

4 small Golden Delicious apples, peeled, cored, and thinly sliced

¼ cup finely chopped dried apricots

2 tablespoons fresh lemon juice

2 tablespoons light brown sugar

2 teaspoons flour

½ teaspoon cinnamon

¼ teaspoon nutmeg

4 reduced-fat refrigerated buttermilk biscuits

1. Preheat oven to 400 degrees F. Coat a large jelly-roll pan with nonstick cooking spray.

2. In a medium bowl, combine apples, dried apricots, lemon juice, sugar, flour, cinnamon, and nutmeg. Toss to mix well.

3. Spray a flat work surface with nonstick cooking spray. Roll out each biscuit or press with fingertips into a 6-inch circle. Place circles on jelly-roll pan. Prick dough in several places with tines of a fork.

4. Divide apple mixture evenly among dough circles, leaving a ¼-inch margin around the edges. Bake 12 to 15 minutes, until crust is golden and apples are just tender.

PER SERVING   Calories 160   Total Fat 1 g   Saturated Fat <1 g
Cholesterol 0 mg   Percentage calories from fat 6%

Spiced Apple-Pear Sauce

Makes 4 servings

This twist on traditional applesauce uses ripe pears in combination with apples for added interest. It is good warm and chilled, by itself or with a big dollop of nonfat vanilla yogurt on top.

4 Golden Delicious apples, peeled, cored, and chopped

4 ripe pears, peeled, cored, and chopped

3 tablespoons unsweetened apple juice

3 tablespoons light brown sugar

2 tablespoons fresh lemon juice

1 teaspoon grated lemon zest

½ teaspoon cinnamon

⅛ teaspoon allspice

1. Combine all ingredients in a large saucepan. Cover and bring to a boil. Reduce heat to medium-low and simmer 12 to 15 minutes, stirring occasionally, until fruit is tender.

2. Transfer to a food processor and puree until smooth. If you prefer a chunky sauce, pulse machine until fruit is chopped. Serve warm or cover and refrigerate until chilled.

PER SERVING   Calories 219   Total Fat 1 g   Saturated Fat <1 g
Cholesterol 0 mg   Percentage calories from fat 4%

Berry Parfaits with Banana Sauce

Makes 4 servings

This quick parfait is a real treat in summer, especially when fresh fruit is at its peak. The sauce is also great served over nonfat frozen yogurt.

1 cup thinly sliced strawberries

1 cup blueberries

½ cup raspberries

2 tablespoons orange juice

1 teaspoon confectioners' sugar

¼ cup nonfat vanilla-flavored yogurt

¼ cup nonfat plain yogurt

½ medium banana, thinly sliced

1 tablespoon skim milk

1 teaspoon honey

⅓ cup reduced-fat granola with raisins

2 tablespoons unsweetened shredded coconut

1. In a medium bowl, combine strawberries, blueberries, raspberries, orange juice, and confectioners' sugar.

2. In a blender or food processor, combine vanilla yogurt, plain yogurt, banana, milk, and honey. Process until smooth and creamy. Reserve ¼ cup for topping.

3. Divide half of the berries equally into bottom of 4 dessert dishes. Top with equal amounts of banana-yogurt mixture and granola. Spoon remaining berries equally over sauce. Top each with 1 tablespoon reserved banana sauce and 1½ teaspoons coconut.

PER SERVING   Calories 118   Total Fat 2 g   Saturated Fat 1 g
Cholesterol 1 mg   Percentage calories from fat 15%

Baked Stuffed Pears

Makes 4 servings

*P*ears *are easy to stuff. Just cut them in half and scoop out the cores with a spoon.*

¼ cup currants or raisins

2 tablespoons finely chopped pecans

1 tablespoon firmly packed brown sugar

1 tablespoon reduced-calorie margarine, melted

½ teaspoon cinnamon

4 small pears, peeled, cut in half, and cored

1 tablespoon fresh lemon juice

½ cup orange-pineapple juice

1½ teaspoons cornstarch

1 teaspoon vanilla extract

1. Preheat oven to 375 degrees F. Coat a 10- or 12-inch oval gratin or rectangular baking dish with nonstick cooking spray. In a small bowl, combine currants, pecans, brown sugar, margarine, and cinnamon. Toss to mix well.

2. Place pears, cored sides up, in prepared baking dish. Sprinkle with lemon juice. In a small bowl, combine orange-pineapple juice, cornstarch, and vanilla. Stir until cornstarch is dissolved.

3. Spoon equal amounts of currant mixture into hollows of pear. Pour juice mixture over pears.

4. Bake 12 to 15 minutes, spooning sauce over pears occasionally, until sauce thickens slightly and pears are just tender.

PER SERVING   Calories 198   Total Fat 7 g   Saturated Fat 1 g
Cholesterol 0 mg   Percentage calories from fat 30%

Quick Blueberry-Peach Cobblers

Makes 4 servings

½ cup cinnamon-flavored graham cracker crumbs

2 tablespoons honey-flavored wheat germ

1 tablespoon orange juice

1 tablespoon reduced-calorie margarine, melted

2 medium peaches, thinly sliced

1 cup blueberries

1 teaspoon finely grated orange zest

2 tablespoons sugar

1½ tablespoons quick-cooking tapioca

1. Preheat oven to 325 degrees F. Coat 4 (6-ounce) custard cups with nonstick cooking spray. Place cups on a baking sheet.

2. In a small bowl, combine cracker crumbs, wheat germ, orange juice, and margarine. In a medium bowl, combine peaches, blueberries, and orange zest. Sprinkle sugar and tapioca over fruit and toss to mix thoroughly.

3. Place 1 tablespoon crumb mixture into bottom of each custard cup. Spoon equal amounts of fruit over crumbs. Sprinkle remaining crumbs on top of fruit.

4. Bake cobblers 12 to 15 minutes, until fruit is bubbly and thickened.

PER SERVING   Calories 156   Total Fat 3 g   Saturated Fat 1 g
Cholesterol 0 mg   Percentage calories from fat 19%

Orange-Date Bars

Makes 12 servings

1 cup chopped pitted dates

¼ cup apple juice

1 teaspoon lemon juice

1¼ cups quick-cooking oats

1 cup plus 2 tablespoons flour

½ cup firmly packed brown sugar

½ cup unsalted margarine, melted

1½ teaspoons finely grated orange zest

¾ teaspoon baking soda

¼ teaspoon salt

1. Preheat oven to 375 degrees F. Coat an 8-inch-square baking pan with nonstick cooking spray.

2. In a small saucepan, combine dates, apple juice, and lemon juice. Bring to a boil; remove from heat.

3. In a medium bowl, combine oats, flour, brown sugar, melted margarine, orange zest, baking soda, and salt. Mix until blended and crumbly. Pat half of oat mixture firmly into bottom of baking pan. Top with dates, spreading to make sure dates are evenly spaced over crust. Top with remaining crumbs, pressing down firmly.

4. Bake 12 to 15 minutes, until top is golden brown. Cut into 12 equal pieces.

PER SERVING   Calories 242   Total Fat 8 g   Saturated Fat 2 g
Cholesterol 0 mg   Percentage calories from fat 30%

Pumpkin Pudding Cups
with Graham Crust

Makes 4 servings

These festive desserts are topped with toasted coconut. To toast coconut quickly, place in a heated nonstick skillet and cook over medium-high heat, stirring constantly, 1 to 2 minutes, until golden brown.

5 (2½-inch) squares graham crackers

1 tablespoon reduced-calorie margarine, melted

2 cups nonfat vanilla-flavored yogurt

1 cup canned pumpkin

¼ cup reduced-calorie whipped topping

1 tablespoon honey

½ teaspoon cinnamon

¼ teaspoon nutmeg

1 tablespoon plus 1 teaspoon toasted flaked coconut

1. Grind graham crackers to crumbs in a blender or small food processor. In a small bowl, toss crumbs with melted margarine to moisten evenly. Spoon equal amounts of crumbs into 4 (6-ounce) custard cups and press firmly into bottom of cups. Place cups in freezer to set.

2. Meanwhile, in a medium bowl, combine yogurt, pumpkin, whipped topping, honey, cinnamon, and nutmeg. Whisk to blend well.

3. Spoon equal amounts of pudding into prepared cups. Sprinkle 1 teaspoon coconut on top of each. Serve immediately or refrigerate for later.

PER SERVING   Calories 156   Total Fat 4 g   Saturated Fat 2 g
Cholesterol 2 mg   Percentage calories from fat 20%

Raisin Cake

Makes 8 servings

¾ cup raisins

¾ cup orange juice

4 tablespoons reduced-calorie margarine, melted

¼ cup sugar

1 teaspoon vanilla extract

1 large whole egg, lightly beaten

1 large egg white, lightly beaten

1 cup flour

¾ teaspoon baking soda

¾ teaspoon baking powder

½ teaspoon cinnamon

½ teaspoon pumpkin pie spice

¼ teaspoon salt

1. Preheat oven to 350 degrees F. Coat an 8-inch square baking pan with nonstick cooking spray.

2. In a small bowl, combine raisins, orange juice, melted margarine, sugar, and vanilla. Add whole egg and egg white; mix well.

3. In a large bowl, stir together flour, baking soda, baking powder, cinnamon, pumpkin pie spice, and salt. Add raisin mixture and beat with a wooden spoon just until combined. Scrape batter into baking pan.

4. Bake 15 to 16 minutes, until a toothpick inserted in center comes out clean. Let cool before cutting into squares to serve.

PER SERVING   Calories 172   Total Fat 4 g   Saturated Fat 1 g
Cholesterol 27 mg   Percentage calories from fat 19%

Peanut Fudge Truffles

Makes 12 servings; 24 truffles

Tuck this terrific recipe away in your holiday file. Truffles make a wonderful gift to wrap and give to someone special. To vary the way they look, they can be rolled in confectioners' sugar or finely chopped nuts. If the truffles become too sticky to roll, try spraying your hands with nonstick cooking spray.

½ cup plus 3 tablespoons unsweetened cocoa powder

½ cup nonfat cream cheese (4 ounces), at room temperature

1 tablespoon reduced-fat smooth peanut butter

1 teaspoon vanilla extract

1 cup sifted confectioners' sugar

1. Place 3 tablespoons cocoa powder on a large piece of wax paper.

2. In a medium bowl with electric mixer on medium speed, beat cream cheese briefly to lighten. Beat in peanut butter and vanilla. Gradually beat in confectioners' sugar and remaining cocoa powder. Beat 2 minutes until well blended and smooth.

3. Divide dough into 24 pieces. Drop each piece in reserved cocoa and roll into a small ball. Refrigerate truffles until serving time. Allow 2 truffles per serving.

PER SERVING   Calories 61   Total Fat 1 g   Saturated Fat 1 g
Cholesterol 1 mg   Percentage calories from fat 15%

Old-Fashioned Oatmeal Cookies

Makes 12 servings; 24 cookies

Chewy with oats, studded with golden raisins, and loaded with pure vanilla, these are sure to be a hit. Serve with coffee, tea, milk, or hot chocolate.

1 cup plus 2 tablespoons quick-cooking oats
⅔ cup flour
½ cup golden raisins
¼ teaspoon cinnamon
¼ teaspoon baking soda
4 tablespoons margarine (not reduced-calorie), softened
¼ cup firmly packed dark brown sugar
2 tablespoons granulated sugar
2 large eggs
1½ teaspoons vanilla extract

1. Preheat oven to 350 degrees F. Coat 2 large cookie sheets with nonstick cooking spray or use nonstick pans.

2. In a small bowl, combine oats, flour, raisins, cinnamon, and baking soda. Mix well. In a large bowl with electric mixer on high speed, beat together margarine, brown sugar, and granulated sugar until light and fluffy. Add eggs and vanilla; beat until well blended, 1 to 2 minutes. Add oat mixture and mix just until combined.

3. Drop by rounded teaspoonfuls onto cookie sheets. Bake 8 to 10 minutes, until golden. Remove to a wire rack and let cool. Allow 2 cookies per serving.

PER SERVING   Calories 157   Total Fat 5 g   Saturated Fat 1 g
Cholesterol 35 mg   Percentage calories from fat 30%

Cocoa Crisps

Makes 12 servings; 24 cookies

*G*inger, cinnamon, and allspice pack these thin, crunchy cookies with spicy taste. The added addition of unsweetened cocoa and grated orange zest gives new life to traditional spice cookies.

⅓ cup molasses

4 tablespoons margarine (not reduced-calorie)

¼ cup firmly packed light brown sugar

½ teaspoon cinnamon

½ teaspoon ground ginger

¼ teaspoon allspice

¾ cup plus 2 tablespoons flour

¼ cup unsweetened cocoa powder

1½ teaspoons finely grated orange zest

1 tablespoon granulated sugar

1. Preheat oven to 350 degrees F. In a small saucepan, combine molasses and margarine. Cook over medium-low heat, stirring often, until margarine melts and blends with molasses. Remove from heat.

2. Place brown sugar, cinnamon, ginger, and allspice in a large bowl; toss to combine. Stir in molasses mixture. Beat with an electric mixer on medium speed 1 to 2 minutes, until well blended. Gradually add flour, cocoa powder, and orange zest, beating until combined.

3. Shape dough into 24 balls about ¾ inch in diameter. Roll each ball in sugar. Place balls on large ungreased baking sheets. Spray bottom of a small glass with nonstick cooking spray. Flatten cookies with bottom of glass.

4. Bake 8 to 10 minutes, until edges start to brown. Let stand on baking sheets 5 minutes. Remove from sheets and let cool completely on wire racks. Allow 2 cookies per serving.

PER SERVING   Calories 118   Total Fat 4 g   Saturated Fat 1 g
Cholesterol 0 mg   Percentage calories from fat 30%

Sweet Noodle Pudding

Makes 4 servings

*M*any times, noodle puddings are found on holiday tables. This quick version will make its way, warm or cold, to your table not just on holidays, but any time a special homemade treat is wanted.

3 cups wide no-yolk noodles

1 large apple, peeled, cored, and diced

½ cup golden raisins

3 tablespoons reduced-calorie margarine, melted

½ cup fruit-flavored nonfat cottage cheese

½ cup egg substitute

2 tablespoons honey

½ teaspoon cinnamon

⅛ teaspoon nutmeg

1 teaspoon granulated brown sugar or regular granulated sugar

1. Preheat oven to 375 degrees F. In a large saucepan of boiling water, cook noodles until just tender, about 10 minutes.

2. In a large bowl, combine noodles, apples, raisins, and melted margarine. Toss lightly to mix. Add cottage cheese, egg, substitute, honey, cinnamon, and nutmeg. Toss to mix well.

3. Spoon noodle mixture into a nonstick 8-inch-square baking pan. Sprinkle brown sugar over top. Bake 15 to 20 minutes, until top is golden brown and pudding is bubbly.

PER SERVING   Calories 386   Total Fat 6 g   Saturated Fat 1 g
Cholesterol 2 mg   Percentage calories from fat 13%

Menus: Low-Fat Entertaining in a Hurry

With *Low Fat in Nothing Flat,* you don't have to worry about diet, even when company's coming. The same nutritional foods you feed your family every day can create great menus for entertaining—all at or below 30 percent calories from fat. What's more, the time-saving approach makes hosting easier on the cook. All recipes noted below are in the book, with the exception of a few fresh fruits, sorbets, and accompaniments. Menus serve four, unless otherwise stated. An asterisk indicates recipe should be doubled to serve the number indicated.

Superbowl Party for Eight

Garlic Baked Potato Chips, page 33

Chunky Salsa with Feta Cheese, *
served with vegetable dippers and
baked tortilla chips, page 24

Crunchy Chicken Fingers, *
page 31

Cheesy Chili Bean Soup, page 41

Raisin Cake, page 217

✳ ✳ ✳ ✳ ✳ ✳ ✳

Elegant Dinner for Entertaining

Watercress Salad with Feta Cheese,
Bacon Dressing, and Garlic Toasts,
page 56

Filet Mignon with Dried Tomato
Topping, page 114

Sautéed Wild Mushrooms and
Asparagus, page 200

Blue Cheese Cauliflower Puree with
Chives, page 197

Mango or orange sorbet

Peanut Fudge Truffles, page 218

Easy Middle Eastern Entertaining

Savory Lemon Hummus, page 27

Chicken Couscous, page 85

Stir-Fried Greens with Garlic
and Walnuts, page 199

Cocoa Crisps, page 220

✳ ✳ ✳ ✳ ✳ ✳ ✳

Casual Dinner for a Few Good Friends

Mozzarella Tomato Crostini,
page 29

Lemon Caesar Salad, page 54

Spaghettini with Red Clam Sauce,
page 78

Apple-Apricot Tartlets, page 210

✳ ✳ ✳ ✳ ✳ ✳ ✳

Cool Supper for a Hot Summer Night

Spicy Crab Gazpacho, page 44

Oriental Steak Salad with Red Onion
and Mandarin Oranges, page 52, or
Crunchy Chicken Salad, page 49

Berry Parfaits with Banana Sauce,
page 212

Hearty Supper for a Wintry Sunday

Chicken Barley Soup, page 42

Cranberry-Apple Pork Chops Braised with Red and Green Cabbage, page 123

Buttermilk Mashed Potatoes, page 201

Broccoli with Creamy Mustard Sauce, page 192

Pumpkin Pudding Cups with Graham Crust, page 216

❁ ❁ ❁ ❁ ❁ ❁ ❁ ❁

Weekend Brunch for Six

Creamy Banana Shake, page 22, or freshly squeezed orange juice

Fruit-Filled Mini Muffins, page 36

Prosciutto and Potato Frittata, page 179

Chicken Ratatouille, page 173

Spiced Apple-Pear Sauce, page 211

Asian Banquet for Eight

Chive Pancakes with Dipping Sauce, page 32

Chicken Egg Rolls, page 96

Spicy Kung Pao Pork, page 122*

Ginger-Glazed Chicken Wings, page 94*

Ham and Egg Fried Rice, page 184, or steamed rice

Orange-Date Bars, page 215, or canned lychees and loquats

❁ ❁ ❁ ❁ ❁ ❁ ❁

Perfect Picnic Fare for Eight to Ten

White Bean and Pepper Dip, page 26, served with fresh vegetable sticks

Tortellini and Shrimp Salad, page 51

Zesty Vegetables Vinaigrette, page 207*

Savory Italian Pie, page 177

Fresh fruit

Old-Fashioned Oatmeal Cookies, page 219

New England Lunch

*Bacon and Chickpea Soup,
page 43*

Broiled Crab Cakes, page 141

*Orange-Pineapple Beets,
page 191*

Crispy Cabbage Slaw, page 194

Cocoa Crisps, page 220

❈ ❈ ❈ ❈ ❈ ❈ ❈

Sit-Down Dinner for Eight

Cheesy Broiled Crostini, page 28

*Vegetable-Stuffed Flank Steak,
page 112*

Spicy Corn Cakes, page 195

*Cheesy Stuffed Tomatoes with Crispy
Topping, page 162*

Baked Stuffed Pears, page 213*

❈ ❈ ❈ ❈ ❈ ❈ ❈

Supper the Kids Will Eat

Crunchy Chicken Fingers, page 31

*Broiled Macaroni and Cheese,
page 69*

*Green Beans with Sunflower Seeds,
page 198*

"Candied" Apples, page 35

Mexican-Style Fiesta for Eight

*South-of-the-Border Vegetable Nachos,
page 30*

*Chunky Salsa with Feta Cheese
(page 24 or store-bought)
and baked tortilla chips*

*Cheese Enchilada Casserole,
page 185*

*Steak Fajitas with Sweet Pepper
Salsa,* page 110*

Barbecued Bean Stew, page 148

*Fresh fruit salad drizzled with honey,
lime juice, and tequila*

❈ ❈ ❈ ❈ ❈ ❈ ❈

Pasta Sampler Buffet for Eight to Ten

*Bow Ties with Bacon and Bread
Crumbs, page 58*

*Tortellini Casserole with Eggplant and
Cheese, page 164*

*Shells with Chunky Meat Sauce, page
76*

*Supper Salad, page 183, or a simple
green salad tossed with low-fat
vinaigrette*

Orange-Date Bars, page 215

Index